I'M THAT GIRL

UNAPOLOGETIC | UNSTOPPABLE

OTTOWEISS COOK

I'm That Girl!

Table Of Contents

UNAPOLOGETIC | UNSTOPPABLE

Introduction

In a world where the voices and potential of women have often been suppressed, this book serves as a beacon of hope and transformation. "I'M THAT GIRL" has been crafted to pave a way for women to stand firm and unyielding, reshaping their futures with unwavering resolve. As God's masterpieces, we embody a newfound power and meaning in becoming unstoppable. I am Ottoweiss F. Cook, a mother to four incredible children—Jedidiah, Samuel, Johnathan, and Jasondra—and the president of Me Mentoring Inc. NFP. My journey has been marked by challenges and triumphs, which I have shared in my previous work, "My Abandoned Heart Ignored." My passion lies in advocating for women, empowering them to break free from the chains that hold them back. "I'M THAT GIRL" is more than a book; it is a declaration of truth and empowerment. Through my own story, I unveil a path to liberation, encouraging women to unmask their true identities and embrace their God-given potential. This book is a call to action, challenging you to rise above the strongholds and step into the fullness of who you are meant to be. Together, we will reshape our tomorrows and redefine what it means to be unstoppable.

UNAPOLOGETIC | UNSTOPPABLE

Foreword

In the tapestry of life, where threads of trials and triumphs intertwine, Ottoweiss Cook emerges – a beacon, a warrior, a healer. She Is the embodiment of grace under fire, a testament to the strength that lies in gentleness, a narrative penned with the ink of resilience. This, beloved, is her declaration, her anthem: "I'm That Girl." As we journey through Ottoweiss's story, where each word dances upon the page like light upon water – illuminating, transforming. Here, in the sacred space between covers, she unfolds the layers of her soul, inviting us into the sanctuary of her experiences, her battles, her victories. "Listen," she whispers, "for in my voice, you'll find echoes of your own." Upon reading, you will quickly find that this is not merely a book; it is a call to arms. Ottoweiss stands, not as a solitary figure, but as a leader in the vanguard of righteousness, battling against the shadows with the sword of truth and the shield of faith. "Don't play with her," for her kindness is her strength, her generosity, her armor. And in her fight, we find the courage to confront our own demons, to stand firm against the winds of injustice. In this literary art we understand that this journey is one of healing, of coming home to oneself. Ottoweiss, through her trials and tribulations, teaches us the art of self-discovery, the beauty of becoming "that girl" who rises from the ashes, who finds power in vulnerability, who crafts beauty from pain. "She can't stand the devil," for her spirit is anointed with the essence of liberation, her heart a wellspring of divine love. So, dear reader, as you turn these pages, let them serve as a mirror reflecting your own potential, your own battles, your own beauty. Let Ottoweiss Cook's story be a beacon guiding you to the truth of who you are and who you are meant to be. For in her narrative, we are all "that girl" – resilient, brilliant, divine. Together, let us embark on this journey of self-discovery, of transformation, of empowerment. For in embracing our stories, we find our strength, our purpose, our light.

Robert H. Marshall Jr. Ed.d
Author of Echoes The Stories of Male Survivors Overcoming Sexual Trauma
CEO, Marshall Enterprise
Chicago, IL

UNAPOLOGETIC | UNSTOPPABLE

Chapter One

I'm Not That Girl, I'm *That* Girl.

I wanted to write "I'm That Girl" to demonstrate this wisdom available to all women—a wisdom that goes far beyond race, culture, and background, and offers a universal message of empowerment and self-discovery. I felt the need to highlight the challenges we face as women but also offer insight to help stir your hearts and rise above those challenges to become a better, stronger woman—a woman who wins, and a woman who becomes unstoppable. As women, we must realize that we are God's creation, we house immense creativity and potential, which many of us never fully unlock. We must take the limits off of ourselves first and then learn to embrace all of the possibilities that are within us. Too often, we smother our potential because of insecurities, self-doubt, and the burdens of societal expectations that hold us back. But remember, you define yourself; do not allow others to do that for you. The journey to self-definition is a powerful one, where you reclaim your identity, voice, and purpose. In the process of defining ourselves, we must also confront the ways in which we tend to distort our God-given image by allowing all of life's hardships to dictate our path. Many times, we find ourselves defeated, and enslaved to circumstances that have wounded our hearts, altered our personalities, and made us faint of heart. But don't be that girl who gives up easily. Instead, be the woman who refuses to be defined by her past, who refuses to let pain or disappointment rob her of her future. Become that high-level woman, leader, entrepreneur, a woman of influence, who dares to dream bigger, push harder, and reach higher. This book encourages you to recover all that has been stolen from you—including your dignity, your self-esteem, and your dreams. Take bold leaps of faith and seek restoration for yourself in all aspects of life. Be unapologetic about your journey. All eyes are on us, women. Let's give the world something to look at by accomplishing bigger and better things while leaving a legacy with footprints that our daughters, nieces, and other women can follow. Every step you take on this journey is a testament to your perseverance, a message to the world that you are not only surviving but thriving. When trying to understand what it means to be "THAT girl," it helps to distinguish between the negative stereotypes that are usually imposed on women and the empowered reality we strive for. These stereotypes are limiting and damaging, reducing women to one-dimensional caricatures rather than acknowledging their full humanity. These generalizations and stereotypes have been used to keep women in boxes and to limit our expression and our capabilities. One pervasive stereotype is the "nagging wife" or "overbearing girlfriend," which unfairly portrays women as excessively demanding and critical. This stereotype undermines women's valid expressions of needs and concerns within relationships, framing them as unreasonable rather than emphasizing the importance of mutual respect and communication. Another harmful stereotype is the "catty woman" narrative, suggesting that women are inherently competitive and jealous of one another. This narrative discourages female solidarity and collaboration, implying that women cannot be trusted to support each other. It fuels a divisive mentality that prevents the formation of strong, empowering networks among women. We must actively reject this narrative by celebrating each other's successes, by lifting each other up, and by recognizing that another woman's success does not have to diminish our own. The "damsel in distress" is another classic stereotype that paints women as helpless and in constant need of rescue. This narrative devalues women's capabilities and reinforces a narrative of dependency, ignoring the strength and resourcefulness women consistently demonstrate in facing life's challenges. Additionally, the "superwoman" stereotype, while seemingly positive, places unrealistic expectations on women to excel in all areas of life without showing any signs of struggle or fatigue. This ideal is completely unattainable and can lead to burnout and feelings of inadequacy when women inevitably fall short of this impossible standard. In contrast to the empowered woman, we aspire to be, there are examples of women who, at their core, do not embody positive qualities. These women may be manipulative, deceitful, or fundamentally lacking in integrity. For instance, the "mean girl" who gets pleasure from belittling others, creating toxic environments wherever she goes. Her actions are rooted in insecurity and a desire to elevate herself by putting others down. Another example is the "gold digger," a woman who prioritizes material wealth and status over genuine connections. She manipulates relationships for personal gain, often leaving a trail of broken hearts and broken trust in her wake. Her focus on superficial success blinds her to the deeper, more fulfilling aspects of life. Then there is the "backstabber," a woman who pretends to be supportive and friendly while secretly undermining others to advance her own position. Her lack of loyalty and integrity destroys trust and creates an atmosphere of suspicion and hostility. These examples serve as reminders of what we must strive to avoid. To be "THAT girl" is to rise above such negative traits and to embody strength, tenacity, and integrity. It means rejecting the superficial and embracing the substantial. It's about understanding that true power comes not from manipulation, but from genuine connection, not from competition, but from collaboration. Positive stereotypes of women can reshape the narrative to celebrate their strengths and potential. The "nurturer" acknowledges women's capacity for empathy, care, and emotional intelligence. These traits are invaluable in personal relationships and professional environments, fostering strong, supportive communities. The "leader" stereotype embraces women's ability to lead with compassion and endurance. Women in leadership roles often bring unique perspectives and solutions, driving innovation and positive change within organizations and society at large. The "innovator" demonstrates women's creativity and problem-solving skills. Throughout history, women have made groundbreaking contributions to science, technology, arts, and humanities, often overcoming significant barriers in doing so. The "warrior" recognizes women's strength and determination in fighting for their rights and the rights of others. This narrative honors women's roles in social justice movements, advocating for equality and systemic change. Being "THAT girl" means embodying strength, resilience, and authenticity. It's recognizing your worth and stepping into your power without any apologies to anyone. "THAT girl" understands that her value is inherent and not defined by society or its standards. She knows her worth is not found in or represented by any outside validation but by an inner confidence that radiates outward. "THAT girl" faces challenges head-on. She understands that adversity is a part of life, but it does not define her. Instead, she uses obstacles as stepping stones to reach higher ground. She is relentless in her pursuit of excellence, constantly pushing boundaries and shattering glass ceilings. "THAT girl" has to be unapologetic about her ambitions. She sets high goals and goes after them with unwavering determination. She is not afraid to take up space and demand what she deserves. Her journey is not without hardships, but she remains steadfast, knowing that every setback is a setup for a greater comeback. "THAT girl" builds and nurtures meaningful connections. She uplifts other women, recognizing that only when coming together, are they stronger. She is a mentor, a friend, and a leader who inspires others to rise above their circumstances and reach their fullest potential. Ultimately, "THAT girl" leaves a legacy. Her footprints are imprinted on the hearts of those she touches, and her impact reverberates through the generations. She is a testament to the power of persistence, the beauty of originality, and the importance of living a life true to yourself. "THAT Girl" does not judge herself or others harshly. She has obtained self-acceptance and has become self-approved. She knows it's okay to be honest with herself, it's okay to admit fears, faults, and failures. She is just fully determined to fulfill her destiny. She refuses to stay stuck. She knows it's okay to not be okay, as long as she gets the help she needs to come out of that space. She does not befriend isolation and become subservient. A few things to remember as well before you presume to claim that title and persona of being "THAT" girl, that positioning comes with a level of responsibility. You have to walk sure. You must be more than confident; you must be certain of who you are and where you are going. When you start behaving and living out your purpose as THAT girl, people will look to you for answers. Women will look up to you to guide them to that place of security. You have to take extra care of your mind body and soul, because you become a beacon for other women, and an example of strength and wisdom that they will turn to in times of uncertainty in their lives. We cannot hold others up if we are not right all the way around, through and through. Let me distinguish this early in the first chapter of this book because it needs to be completely understood before we go any further. I realize that if you are reading this with the wrong mindset, all of this, the entire premise of this project can come across as arrogance or me being too full of myself or conceited. It is so important to distinguish the difference between confidence and arrogance. This is part of a huge problem with women today. We are afraid to be our true selves and walk in such certainty for fear of being judged as "stuck up" or narcissistic. The whole idea and concept that I am trying to convey in this book will be lost on most, unfortunately, because we are conditioned to hide our boldness when it threatens the security of others. I am here to help you BREAK that way of thinking. There is nothing wrong with being happy with yourself or loving who you are. There is nothing wrong with exuding confidence and liking who you see in the mirror looking back at you. That is how backward we have this thing. Why does my confidence have to threaten anyone else's? It does not. I did not choose to write this whole book just to tell you about how great I am. And if you read this and are led to that notion, you got to check your heart and begin to reassess your way of thinking. It probably is not even your fault that you may think so negatively. As I said, we have been conditioned to think WRONG. You can be humble and still be THAT girl. In fact, that is one of the traits that being THAT girl requires. You can be assertive and confident without being extra, loud, or boisterous, constantly bragging about yourself. If you don't get anything else in this entire book, please get this: Confidence is about having a healthy sense of self-assurance and trust in your abilities and worth. Key word being healthy. It's about knowing who you are, what you stand for, and being comfortable in your own skin. Confident people should be seen as positive, inspiring, and approachable. They don't need to put others down to feel good about themselves; instead, they lift others up and create an environment of mutual respect and encouragement. On the other hand, cockiness, arrogance, and conceit are often rooted in insecurity and an unhealthy need to prove yourself. Cocky individuals tend to overestimate their abilities and often come across as boastful and dismissive of others and their qualities.

Arrogance requires a sense of superiority and entitlement, while conceit is an excessive pride in yourself. These traits can alienate others and create a negative atmosphere. Now, when it comes to women, there's a societal double standard that often comes into play. Many women are hesitant to openly display confidence or pride in their achievements because they fear being labeled as cocky, arrogant, or conceited. That fear is rooted in cultural norms and stereotypes that have historically placed women in more submissive roles. Women who are confident and assertive are too often unfairly judged and criticized more harshly than their male counterparts, which usually leads to fear and reluctance to showcase their strengths and accomplishments, which in turn will hinder their personal and professional growth. We have to continuously challenge these stereotypes and encourage women to embrace their confidence and be proud of who they are. Confidence in women should be celebrated and seen as a positive trait that contributes to their success and well-being. When we support and uplift each other, we create a more inclusive and empowering environment where everyone feels free to be their authentic selves. Remember, being confident doesn't mean you have to be perfect or have all the answers. It's about being true to yourself, acknowledging your strengths and weaknesses, and always striving for growth. How do we fix this narrative and way of thinking so that we are NOT judging and treating other women with confidence unfairly? This is a systemic, generational problem that will not be fixed with just one conversation, or one chapter in a book. We got to start in our own circles first. We have to start having these conversations within our inner circles and communities. The ignorance in thinking you understand these labels and what they mean, then using them against our friends or strangers is part of the problem. Now I have explained the difference between these words, so now that you personally have read and understand the difference, you must do better. Next time you see a woman walking in complete certainty of herself, and she has a light shining from within, don't talk bad about her to others. Don't dim her light by spreading the narrative that she is stuck up or conceited. That is how it starts, with whispers in each other's ears, and texts behind others' backs filled with judgment and insults. Change the narrative. Celebrate her to others, use her as an example for your own life. Instead of warning others about her confidence, try and get as close as you can to her, because we can always learn from one another. And maybe, just maybe, her light will inspire you to shine your own! I had to explain all of that because I know from experience how misunderstood you can be when you walk through life as THAT girl. More often than not, that confidence is completely misinterpreted because folks simply are ignorant and don't understand it. People tend to act out negatively when they do not understand something. My confidence has had that negative effect on people so many times. Women will see me and put their noses in the air thinking, "Who does she think she is?" Well, let me tell you... I AM THAT GIRL! You can be too! That is the purpose of this book. Not to brag to you about my many awesome qualities as a woman/leader/entrepreneur, but to inspire you to be and feel the same way about yourself. Again, there is a level of responsibility to educate and empower when you assume the role of THAT girl. There is an obligation to be a voice for the voiceless and a duty to help others find and use their voice. Being THAT girl means being a role model and advocating for things that matter. Being THAT girl means inspiring unity and togetherness. It means constantly learning and growing and continuous self-improvement. It means handling criticism and hateful accusations with grace and forgiveness. It also means building and maintaining strong supportive relationships. It does not mean being perfect at everything you try to do. Perfection has nothing to do with striving and persevering toward excellence in all things. It means being constantly misjudged and misunderstood but choosing to educate with love and grace rather than becoming bitter. It means seeing someone hurting and reaching a hand out to help them, regardless of who they are or where they come from. It means being okay with not knowing everything all the time but willing to learn at all times. Being THAT girl means being someone that your community can look up to, even if you do not have all the answers, you are willing to figure it out, for the greater good. It means putting how you feel in the moment aside, to get what needs to be done, done. Perseverance is key. It is being able to admit when you are wrong and being willing to take the steps to make whatever "it" is, right. I pray that you, whoever you are that is reading this now, that you hear my heart's desire in these pages. I pray you don't misjudge or misinterpret. I pray you don't attack my confidence because you might be lacking your own. My ultimate hope is that you are able to fully understand that I wrote this with you in mind, anticipating that you will utilize the wisdom in this book to learn how to shine your own light for all to see. Try to listen with your heart and not your intellect. And, as you journey through the pages of "I'M THAT GIRL," may you be inspired to embrace your own path with courage and conviction. Let this book be a guide, a source of strength, and a reminder that you, too, can be THAT girl–unstoppable, unapologetic, and undeniably powerful. The wisdom and empowerment within these pages are yours to claim. Step into your greatness, and let your life be the living proof that you are, indeed, THAT girl.

Chapter Two

True Identity

In today's digital age, the concept of identity and being true to yourself is becoming more and more difficult. Every day, we go online and see others flaunting these projected identities, in an attempt to be accepted and loved. Social media platforms like Instagram, Facebook, and TikTok are filled with influencers and celebrities who set unrealistic standards for beauty, success, and lifestyle. From the moment we wake up until we go to sleep, we are engulfed in a never-ending cycle of comparison. How can we truly know and accept ourselves if we are constantly comparing what we have to others? This "influencer era" seems to be causing more harm than good, especially for younger people just starting out their lives as adults. They see peers their age making obscene amounts of money and gaining fame by presenting what looks like a perfectly put-together life in a 15-second video or an Instagram image with a carefully crafted caption. Please, ladies, keep in mind that most of what is put online is literally just a tiny piece of someone's day, and most of what you see online is not real life. It is entertainment. Your identity is not found in views, likes, or even in financial success. We have lost touch with finding and owning our unique qualities and passions, adopting the personas and lifestyles we see and portray online instead. The meaning of success is now measured by views and comments rather than meaningful memories and personal talents. People strive to perfect their online personas instead of becoming genuinely good human beings. We really need to take a closer look at this because many of our identities are now limited to our online profiles, leaving us with less to offer in real-life interactions.

People often showcase their online presence to reflect a certain image or character, which is rarely entirely authentic. We show our "best" selves online only the best selfies, best meals, best vacation moments, and so on. In doing so, we have abandoned the need for self-discovery and rely on the mask of social media to express who we truly are. Understanding your true identity is of paramount importance. The road leading you to that understanding is equally important. For us women, self-awareness is perhaps the most rewarding gift we can give ourselves. I emphasize this because I see so many women grappling with self-identification and identity crises. That struggle usually leads to a distorted sense of existence, causing many women to morph into someone or something they are not. By the age of 10, I realized I had this level of awareness of myself. This is another example of the many special gifts God gave me. In my life, I have walked SURE, knowing deep in my heart that I was chosen by God. When you understand your value and are confident in who you are, there will always be a challenge to your confidence. People, situations, and the biggest challenge will be matters of your own heart. Also remember that your adversary knows you, your strengths and weaknesses, and will always look for a foothold to break you and his job is to take you out. So, for me personally, in my life, I genuinely have not struggled with knowing who I am. Now, I do discuss this in another chapter briefly, and I go even more in-depth about this in my previous book. There was a time when I strayed away from myself. Don't get me wrong, I always knew who I was and who I was created to be, again, since 10 years old I have been completely certain. But as a result of consistently being mistreated and rejected by my family, that pain manifested and took me down a road where I could have lost myself. I thank God that I was able to catch it quickly and that I came to an understanding within myself to not let anyone ever cause me to change who I am to force them to accept me or show me, love. That is a lie from Hell ladies. It is a very dangerous road to go down, one that can lead to a lifetime of becoming and behaving completely out of character and ultimately activate a storm of confusion within yourself. When you refuse to embrace who you are and try to change to fit others' perception of you, there is no peace to be found for you there in that place. When I went through that time that I was trying to be someone else, I ended up surrounded by people who did not enhance the quality of my life but rather made it chaotic and full of disorder and mess. I am grateful that God has given me this assurance, on the inside, otherwise I would be cleaning up after that mess for the rest of my life. When you are trying to be someone you're not, it will become harder and harder for you to sit with yourself, and look at yourself in the mirror, and you will always be making choices that have real negative consequences. Let me explain. When I started searching for validation and acceptance in people who didn't align with what I knew to be right, pure, and righteous, I found myself around the troublemakers. I started to become disruptive and disrespectful in school, would insult my teachers, and get into arguments, fighting with everyone all the time. I became someone who was always causing disturbances everywhere I went, I became increasingly angry, and unsettled, had no patience and my whole existence was essentially entangled in a web of dysfunction. Beyond my teenage years when I got a little older, still trying to be someone who I knew I was not at my core, the behavior shifted from juvenile attempts to gain attention to now I was going to dance clubs, dressing somewhat provocatively, trying to look older than I was. I became curious about sex and men and all that comes with that part of life. Let me tell you, an 18-year-old young woman, who was on a mission to completely abandon her true identity, looking for all the wrong kind of attention, and now intrigued by men and sex, that is a perfect recipe for absolute disaster. During this period of my life, I knew deep down who I was supposed to be and who God created me to be, but I chose to go the opposite direction because my heart had become so calloused and rooted in rejection, that I was lost. My heart was severely wounded, and all my decisions reflected that. All I truly yearned for was acceptance, but I just kept trying to be relevant and fit in, all the while abandoning my true identity, and the purpose God had for my life. The further I got away from my true identity and my calling, the more uncomfortable I became. The level of conviction I experienced while hanging around the wrong crowd, and things that didn't align with my spirit, just increased more and more until I had enough. As a result of this period of not allowing my true self to prevail, I had gotten pregnant with my first child. This was sort of an awakening for me, I became a mom and wanted my child to feel and have all of the love and everything I had been lacking, so it made me change my thinking. I had to start fighting vigorously for myself and my identity. I thank God that he never really allowed me to fully walk away from myself and Him. The emotional scars were deep from all that I have had to endure, but I have continued to press on. I have faced many storms, but I've weathered those storms through my intimate prayer life, holding on to a grace unmatched, a grace given to me by God. We have to learn the importance of practicing mindfulness, and continuously making ourselves aware of how God sees us. The Bible provides profound insights into our identity and purpose. According to Scripture, we are created in the image of God, which is foundational to understanding our true identity. Genesis 1:27 says, "God created mankind in his own image." This verse tells us that our worth and identity are inherently tied to our divine creator. Being created in God's image means that we possess a natural dignity, value, and purpose. It signifies that we reflect Godly attributes such as love, wisdom, creativity, and the capacity for solid relationships. Psalm 139:13-14 beautifully articulates the intentionality and care with which we were created: "For you created my inmost being; you knit me together in my mother's womb. I praise you because I am fearfully and wonderfully made; your works are wonderful; I know that full well." Reading, studying, fully comprehending and living out what the bible says about us is so powerful. Those passages, explain how our existence is not an accident but a deliberate act of divine craftsmanship. We are intricately designed, each with unique qualities and purposes. Your identity is not represented by the trials you've faced, but rather, by how you've risen above them. We have to spend time with ourselves, to fall in love with who we truly are. The relationship with yourself forms the cornerstone of a strong, solid identity. It is through moments of solitude and introspection that you can connect with your inner thoughts, fears, wants, and needs. Journaling, quiet time with yourself, or even sometimes spending time in nature can be amazing tools for discovering what you don't know or understand about yourself. By understanding your likes, dislikes, values, and aspirations, you begin to paint a clear picture of who you are at your core. Once you comprehend your true identity, you can begin to heal from the wounds that have been inflicted on you by life's trials. Those wounds can stem from different things- sexual assault, molestation, failed marriages, toxic relationships, abandonment, verbal abuse, or even the profound loneliness of being orphaned. Those damaging experiences can leave deep scars, making it difficult to recognize and accept your true self. Each of these traumatic experiences can impact a woman's self-esteem and sense of worth. Sexual assault and molestation, for instance, can incite feelings of shame, guilt, and unworthiness. Failed marriages and toxic relationships can lead to a loss of trust and fear of intimacy. Abandonment, whether physical or emotional, can generate a deep-seated fear of rejection and loneliness. Verbal abuse can disintegrate your self-confidence and instill a sense of inadequacy. The loneliness of being orphaned can foster a sense of isolation and disconnection from the world. All these things can lead to spiritual confusion, where we lose touch with our true selves. When we do lose touch with ourselves, we compromise our entire fundamental nature, leaving us feeling lost and disconnected. Then comes spiritual disarray, leaving us in a state where our souls are in turmoil due to unresolved trauma and suppressed emotions. In many cultures, spiritual confusion or disarray is seen as a crisis of the soul, where the individual feels disconnected from their purpose and inner truth. When I went through that time in my life when I was living in rebellion of my true self, my heart, mind, and soul were in a state of complete disarray. I knew I was headed in a direction that was further and further away from my destiny. I still knew myself and my purpose, but I was disconnected from that inner truth, and it was becoming more and more distorted. Just lost. Think about being adrift in a vast, uncharted ocean, without a compass to guide you. Reconnecting with your spiritual essence involves diving deep into your inner world, confronting the darkness within, and emerging with a renewed sense of clarity and purpose. Knowing and accepting your true identity is also recognizing your strength, resilience, and the unique qualities that make you who you are. Your experiences shape you, but they do not determine your worth or what you are capable of. Each challenge you overcome adds to your reservoir of strength and wisdom, enabling you to navigate future obstacles with greater resistance. When focusing on self-discovery, you must confront any painful experiences you have faced, understand them, and ultimately, move beyond them. Confronting these things will allow you to reclaim your identity, understand your worth, and embrace the person you truly are on the inside. Confronting these experiences can be very scary, but it is a necessary step toward healing. I need you to know and understand this: healing is possible, no matter how scary and impossible it may seem to you. I know a lot of times when facing these things that intimidate us, we choose to try and ignore or act like the things we need to heal from are not significantly affecting us, and that they don't matter. I am here to tell you that they do! Especially when trying to figure out who you are and become the best version of yourself. There is no way to do that unless we boldly address what has hurt us in the past.   Remember, your identity is your power. It's the foundation upon which you build your life, and it's the compass that guides you on your journey. Cherish it, nurture it, and most importantly, never let it go. Throughout my life, despite the many hurts and times of heartache, I have perfected the act of loving and accepting myself. Even that truth-loving myself in spite of everything life has thrown my way, seems to trigger others to be intimidated by my confidence and my stance toward myself. People will always try and alter your identity to fit their expectations, but I've been able to remain steadfast and unmovable in knowing self. Fully embracing your identity requires accepting all aspects of yourself –your past hurts, your strengths, weaknesses, quirks, and imperfections. We got to stop living in denial about the aspects of our lives and ourselves that aren't always 'pretty'. Nobody expects you or your life to be perfect, that is such a terrible way to live. Bad things happen, a lot of times to the best of us. When we accept that we have all been through things that we may not be especially proud of, only then do we experience real freedom. Our flaws and mistakes help us relate to each other and your testimony; your truth may just be the thing that someone needs to hear to begin the healing they need for their lives. We got to welcome and accept those 'ugly' experiences to become THAT girl. Being THAT girl means celebrating your uniqueness and standing confidently in your truth. When women look inward, they tend to judge themselves and only focus on their weaknesses, overlooking their strengths. It is truly eye-opening to realize that our strengths and weaknesses together shape our identity. They are the yin and yang of our existence, each complementing the other. Our strengths propel us forward, while our weaknesses keep us grounded, reminding us of our humanity. Strengths are not just our talents or skills; they are also our morals, and our motivations. They are what make us feel alive, energized, and fulfilled. On the other hand, our weaknesses are not just our flaws or shortcomings; they are our challenges, our opportunities for growth and learning. Identifying and understanding the significance of our strengths and weaknesses combined allows us to create a balanced, authentic life. It enables us to leverage our strengths to pursue our dreams and to use our weaknesses as a springboard toward personal growth. Authenticity empowers us to make choices that align with our true selves, leading to a life of fulfillment and happiness. When we live authentically, we attract people and opportunities that only resonate with our true selves, creating a life that is in harmony with our principles and what genuinely makes us happy. Authenticity nurtures genuine connections and deepens our relationships because most people are drawn to honesty and integrity. Authenticity also requires vulnerability, because it causes us to show our real selves, imperfections, and all. Vulnerability is a source of strength, it promotes deeper, more meaningful connections with others. When we are authentic, we are more likely to attract people who appreciate and respect us for who we actually are, rather than for the mask we might present to the world. Once you've discovered your true identity and embraced your strengths and weaknesses, you are well-equipped to create the life you want and need. Let's shift the conversation a little to another aspect of women knowing and becoming their unique selves regardless of what the world expects from us. The journey to self-identification is full of challenges. Let's face it; women face pressures from society, cultural expectations, and personal insecurities that cause them to hide themselves. These outside influences and internal battles will lead to a fractured sense of identity, where the woman feels compelled to conform to roles and expectations that do not resonate with her authentic self. This is a dilemma that often results in emotional and mental distress, making it necessary to begin on that path to self-discovery. Throughout history, women have always been expected to fit a specific construct, created by a male-dominated social system. These expectations destroy a woman's individuality and creativity, forcing her into a mold that doesn't fit her true nature. The pressure to fulfill roles like; the perfect daughter, wife, mother, or professional can lead to an inner conflict, where our desires and the expectations society has established for us clash. That battle within causes many women to lose sight of their true identity and then they feel a deep sense of dissatisfaction and loss. Creating and chasing after the life you want also means setting clear, meaningful goals that align with your identity and your core values. It requires courage to pursue these goals, resilience to overcome obstacles, and perseverance to keep going despite setbacks. The life you want means envisioning your ideal future and setting goals that reflect your true desires and passions. These goals should be specific, measurable, achievable, relevant, and time-bound (SMART). Break them down into smaller, manageable steps and celebrate your progress along the way. Having that approach keeps you motivated and focused, making your dreams more attainable. For example, if your goal is to pursue a career that aligns with your passion, start by identifying what excites and motivates you. Research potential career paths, acquire the necessary skills or education, and build a network of supportive people who can guide and mentor you. By taking consistent, purposeful steps toward your goal, you move closer to creating a life that reflects your true identity. Creating the life you want also means setting boundaries and prioritizing self-care. Respecting your own needs and feelings will encourage you to make time for activities that nourish your soul. Self-care is not a luxury; it is a necessity. It means taking care of your physical, emotional, and mental well-being through things like regular exercise, healthy eating, adequate rest, and engaging in hobbies that bring you joy. Setting boundaries and sticking to them is life-changing This means learning to say no to demands that drain you and yes to opportunities that align with your passions. Boundaries help you manage your time and energy effectively, ensuring that you have the resources to pursue your goals and maintain your well-being. We should be building healthy relationships that uplift and distance ourselves from toxic influences. Surround yourself with people who support and encourage you, and who respect your boundaries and beliefs. Healthy relationships have to be based on mutual respect, trust, and open communication. Healthy relationships provide a safe space for you to be your authentic self and to grow and thrive. Building those healthy relationships also involves recognizing and addressing any toxic dynamics in your current relationships. This means having difficult conversations, setting firm boundaries, or, in some cases, separating yourself from individuals who do not respect or support you. By cultivating a supportive and positive social network, you create an environment that nurtures your growth and well-being. One thing I want to be clear on throughout this book is the absolute importance of self-perception. Many aspects of being "THAT Girl" stem from how we view ourselves and what we do with what we like and dislike when we do discover those things about us. Understanding your true identity has an absolute level of certainty to it. Being sure of who you are, comes with confidence; there is no way around it. Not cockiness or conceitedness, no, that is something else entirely. When you have done the work on yourself, searched inside your soul to see what it is that makes you, you; insecurity and low self-esteem have no place anymore because you have worked through your trauma and gone past the pain to find the truth. Feeling insecure and having low self-esteem often comes from not being confident and feeling unsure about yourself. These feelings can pile up and make you feel inadequate, anxious, and worried, which can show up as tiredness, intrusive thoughts, and even fears like separation anxiety. When you're not sure or anxious about who you are, it's easy to be hard on yourself, leading to nervousness, dread, and a restless mind. But the journey to finding and loving your true self starts with self-acceptance. This means acknowledging every part of yourself, even the parts that need improvement, and practicing self-approval. It's about digging deep to truly understand your worth and recognizing that failure or lack of success doesn't define you. Instead, accepting yourself with all your strengths and weaknesses is the key to overcoming insecurity and building genuine self-esteem. This process of digging deep to find and understand yourself fully helps you create and maintain a more peaceful, focused mind and discover who you really are at your core. Remember, the journey to self-discovery and self-love is not a destination, but a continuous process. It's a path of growth, learning, and transformation. And as you walk this path, remember to celebrate each step, each discovery, each victory. Each step brings you closer to your true self, each discovery reveals a new component of your identity, and each victory strengthens your love for yourself.

Chapter Three
Fearlessly Breaking Barriers

When I began thinking about fearlessness, I paused—because fear has always been an abstract concept to me. I've never really been afraid, yet I understand that fear can be a powerful force in our lives, especially for women. Often ingrained by society, fear limits our potential and confines us to traditional roles and expectations. From a young age, women are conditioned to adhere to certain roles, which can stifle our true potential. Fear of stepping outside these boundaries—whether pursuing a career, speaking up in a relationship, or being true to yourself—can be overwhelming. Yet, it's in these moments of fear that we find our strength. Fearlessness isn't about the absence of fear but the courage to move forward despite it. What if we viewed fear not as an enemy but as a catalyst for change? What if fear drove us to break down barriers? It's about confronting insecurities, questioning the status quo, and rising above limitations. Fearlessness calls us to reclaim our power and rewrite the narratives handed down to us. The journey to fearlessness isn't solitary; it's cultivated within communities of women who support, uplift, and inspire each other. When viewed this way, fear becomes a teacher rather than an enemy. Together, we can challenge society's expectations, defy toxic traditions, and create a collective strength that breaks barriers. Vulnerability plays a valuable role. Admitting our fears, seeking help, and accepting our true selves connects us to others and builds the toughness needed to overcome obstacles. It takes immense courage to admit when we're afraid, acknowledge our doubts, and seek help. In our vulnerability, we find connection and strength. By practicing vulnerability, we allow others to see our true selves, fostering deeper relationships and creating spaces where fear has no power. This journey of welcoming our fears and taking bold steps to break barriers is deeply personal and spiritual. It requires introspection and a strong connection to our faith. By diving into scripture, praying for guidance, and seeking wisdom in those quiet moments, we build an unshakable foundation that allows us to stand firm in the face of fear. The Bible teaches us that God's love casts out all fear (1 John 4:18). This profound truth reminds us that, with faith, we are never really alone, and fear can never truly hold us back unless we allow it to. There is a scripture in 2 Timothy that states we have not been given a spirit of fear but of power, love, and a sound mind—a truth we must actively commit to living by. Throughout my life, I have realized that fear has no place in it. The Bible gives us wisdom and knowledge to live by, to live our best life, and to live righteously in God's eyes. Our lives are mapped out for us; the script has already been written. Fear isn't merely an emotion; it's a primal survival mechanism. Our ancestors relied on fear to avoid predators and navigate treacherous landscapes. But in today's complex world, fear takes on new forms. It creeps into our minds when we face challenges, uncertainties, or the unknown. It whispers, "What if you fail?" or "What if they reject you? " Fear hijacks our brain, triggering the amygdala—the ancient alarm system. Our rational thinking takes a backseat as adrenaline surges through our veins. When that alarm gets triggered, our human nature tells us to fight or flee. But often, fear will paralyze us. Sometimes we react impulsively, damaging relationships or missing opportunities. Fear wears many masks: Fear of Failure: The fear that our efforts won't measure up, that we'll stumble and fall. Fear of Rejection: The dread of not being accepted, loved, or valued. Fear of the Unknown: The uncertainty that keeps us awake at night, wondering what lies ahead. By understanding the science of fear and comparing it to what the Bible says, we find the tools to overcome it. The Bible encourages us to live without fear, to trust in God's plan, and to encompass that spirit of power, love, and a sound mind. Fearlessness should be contagious among women. It puts us in the state of mind of a conqueror, where we can see through a woman's eyes without fearing anything. Living without fear and demonstrating faith allows us to thrive and live our best lives. By recognizing the masks fear wears and understanding its impact on our lives, we can rise above it. We must always remember to break down this thing that is ultimately trying to defeat us. We must think things through so that when we respond, our responses are constructive. When we focus on fear and the things that make us afraid, the remedy is learning how to elevate our faith, which pulls out those feelings of torment. I say torment because fear can absolutely torment us. As women especially, one of our fears is not being able to excel in life. However, we fail to realize that we shape our own destiny with boldness and clarity about the true nature of who we are. We often stay in confused states of mind because we are not daring enough and lack the ambition to flourish. What's hindering you is only you, and that is the ultimate retort you can have for yourself. We create our own paths through vision. We have to see things first in order to start making things happen in our lives. At the heart of overcoming fear lies the power of vision the ability to envision a future defined by purpose and possibility. Conquering fear and embracing faith is not merely a matter of spiritual conviction; it is a testament to the tenacious spirit of the human soul. By anchoring ourselves in the timeless truths of scripture and the boundless power of faith, we can transcend the limitations of fear and embark upon a journey of self-discovery and self-realization. Fear will eat at our hearts and weaken our core. Fear hinders the flow of God in our lives and smothers hope. Women often face unique fears, from societal expectations to personal insecurities. The fear of not being enough–whether as a professional, a mother, or a partner–can be overwhelming. Women possess incredible resilience. We can overcome fears by realizing our strengths and trusting our abilities. Empowerment comes from within, and by supporting each other, we create a community of fearless women who uplift and inspire. Motherhood brings its own set of fears. The responsibility of nurturing and protecting a child can be daunting. Mothers often worry about their children's safety, health, and future. In the night, fear tortures women's minds with the despair that they can't feed their children. However, motherhood also brings immense strength. By leaning on faith and the support of loved ones, mothers navigate these fears with grace. The love for their children becomes a powerful motivator to face and conquer any fear. Christianity teaches us to live without fear, trusting in God's plan and His love for us. The Bible is filled with verses that encourage us to be brave and courageous. By grounding ourselves in these teachings, we find the strength to face our fears. Faith provides a foundation of hope and assurance, reminding us that we are never alone in our struggles. With God by our side, we can overcome any obstacle. Living fearlessly as a woman means surrendering to your true self and stepping into your power. It means rejecting societal norms that try to confine you and instead defining your own path. When you live fearlessly, you become "THAT GIRL"–unapologetically yourself, pursuing your dreams with passion and inspiring others to do the same. Fearlessness is about taking risks and knowing that failure is just a bridge to success. It's about speaking your truth, even when your voice shakes. It's about loving yourself fiercely and knowing your worth. When you live fearlessly, you attract opportunities and people who align with your highest potential. You become a beacon of light, showing others that it is possible to live a life of purpose and joy. Living fearlessly does more than transform your own life; it also creates a domino effect that empowers others to do the same. You become a role model, a leader, and an inspiration. You show that it is possible to live a life without limits, to break free from the chains of fear, and to soar to new heights. We gotta embrace our fearlessness, step into our power, and become "THAT GIRL," who lives her best life with courage, fearlessness, and grace. Even if you are afraid, do it anyway! Do it, afraid. By rising above fear and embracing faith, we unlock our potential to lead lives filled with purpose, strength, and love. Fear is often that invisible force that tugs at our hearts, whispers doubt in our ears, and will cast shadows on our dreams. Still, within us lies the power to defy fear, to live boldly, and to become the epitome of "that girl"—the one who strides through life with unwavering confidence and purpose. Fearlessness is about action. It's not enough to simply acknowledge our fears; we must actively work to overcome them. This might mean taking small steps toward a larger goal, setting boundaries in our personal lives, or making bold decisions that align with our values. Every act of courage, no matter how small, is a step toward living a fearless life. Fearlessness challenges us to confront our insecurities, to question the status quo, and to rise above the limitations imposed upon us. When women come together, share their stories, and support one another, they create a collective strength that can move mountains, break barriers, and create spaces where we can be our true, powerful selves. The voyage to fearlessness does not and should not have to be taken alone. By building and nurturing a community of like-mindedness, we can inspire and empower each other to face our fears head-on. Together, we can break free from the chains that bind us and step into a future defined by possibility and purpose. Breaking barriers is the ultimate expression of fearlessness. It requires us to identify and dismantle the internal and external obstacles that hold us back. As women, we often face societal barriers—gender stereotypes, discrimination, and bias—that limit our opportunities. These barriers are not of our making, yet they profoundly impact our lives. Fearlessness empowers us to challenge these limitations, to advocate for equal treatment, and to demonstrate that our capabilities are not defined by our gender. There are so many barriers we impose on ourselves that must be addressed first. We cannot presume to help anyone or anything unless our proverbial house is in order. We must first confront the internal struggles that hinder us—self-doubt, insecurity, low self-esteem. These are the barriers we often create for ourselves, and they can be the most difficult to overcome. By showcasing fearlessness and fostering a strong connection to our faith, we can transcend these limitations. It seems women face a constant battle to secure a tangible future for themselves. Often, we find ourselves in situations where we must break down barriers and unlock doors that were deliberately shut in our faces by those who seek to suppress us simply because we are women. We are frequently labeled as the weaker vessel, but consider this: that notion is a myth. The world today is framed by women's strength, and our men sometimes need a bit more of a push than we do. We are receivers and go-getters. We are kindhearted, verbally expressive, courageous, fearless, and filled with substance. Without us, I believe the world would descend into greater chaos because we are the heartbeat of God. Our willingness to help those in need is unmatched. Our passion runs deep—I have yet to meet a man whose emotional reservoir matches ours. Think about the strength of a woman: childbirth alone sets us apart, allowing us to carry another human being inside our bodies and bring life into the world. As women, we must stop allowing ourselves to be trapped by the mindset that we have limits. No, we are breaking down those barriers, and we will always position ourselves to win. A woman with determination and a made-up mind is a formidable force in the world. She is simply unstoppable. Removing hindrances from our path requires skill. We must equip ourselves to ensure that we always triumph from within and never allow ourselves to be continually plagued by internal struggles. To overcome what troubles our minds, we must first understand what is hindering us. Barriers can manifest as self-doubt, insecurity, low self-esteem, anger, resentment, and malice. We can assassinate our own character by allowing these negative traits to fester. To break the barriers that imprison us, we must first admit that we are grappling with these issues. Being honest with ourselves elevates us to a different mental capacity, enabling us to tackle our challenges head-on. We often think a single issue holds us back, but in reality, it can be many things. Breaking barriers requires introspection and a commitment to personal growth. We must recognize and dismantle the obstacles we create for ourselves. Only then can we truly break free and achieve the victories we deserve. Discovering our strengths, confronting our weaknesses, and continuing to break barriers will pave the way for a future where we are not just survivors but thrivers, making an indelible impact on the world. Preconceived notions about women's roles and behaviors limit our aspirations and potential by dictating what is 'appropriate' for our gender. Challenging these stereotypes and demonstrating that our capabilities are not defined by gender is essential. Women often face discrimination in various aspects of life, including the workplace, where we may be overlooked for promotions or paid less than our male counterparts for the same work. Overcoming this requires standing up against such injustices and advocating for equal treatment and opportunities. The expectation to manage both professional responsibilities and domestic duties consistently falls disproportionately on women, leading to stress and burnout. Advocating for shared responsibilities at home and flexible work policies is imperative. And remember this: breaking barriers is a perpetual journey requiring immense willpower and unwavering determination. It is not a one-time event but a continuous journey of self-improvement and advocacy. We must be aggressive in the face of adversity, stand up for ourselves and others when faced with injustice, and continually strive for equality and fairness. It's about more than just removing obstacles—it's about redefining what is possible. Fearlessness provides a foundation for breaking down barriers, enabling us to navigate challenges with clarity and purpose. Whether it's overcoming personal fears or dismantling societal constraints, fearlessness gives us the strength to keep moving forward, no matter how formidable the barriers may seem. Every barrier we break creates a ripple effect that extends far beyond ourselves. Our actions, when driven by fearlessness, influence not only our own lives but also the lives of those around us and future generations. As women, we have the power to shape our destiny and the destiny of others. By living fearlessly and breaking down barriers, we create a legacy of empowerment, showing that it is possible to live a life without limits. Each barrier we break paves the way for future generations of women to live their best lives. Remember, every barrier we break and every ceiling we shatter is a step towards creating a world where being a woman is seen as a strength, not a limitation. We are not just breaking barriers for ourselves but for all women. We are THAT GIRL, and we will continue to break barriers and live our best lives. We gotta strive to inspire others to do the same. We are unstoppable. We are women. We are THAT girl. In addition to all of those barriers that I've mentioned, women in the church and Christian faith often face distinctive challenges. Traditional gender roles within the church can limit women's participation and influence. These stereotypes hinder women from fully expressing their faith and contributing to their religious communities. Many churches still restrict women from holding certain leadership positions, limiting the diversity of perspectives within church leadership. Certain interpretations of religious texts are often used to justify the subordination of women, creating barriers for those seeking equality within their faith communities. The contributions of women in the church are often overlooked or undervalued, discouraging active participation. Breaking these barriers requires both individual and collective action. We must challenge traditional gender roles and advocate for equal representation in leadership. Churches must recognize and value the contributions of women and create an environment where all members can fully participate and lead. By breaking these barriers, women can make significant strides towards equality within the church and Christian faith, benefiting not only women but also enriching their faith communities as a whole. We gotta get to a place where our distinct perspectives are seen and valued by everyone. Ladies, let's get up, stand up, and move forward. We have much to obtain, so stumbling blocks must be removed from our path. Seeing a clear path forward requires us to open doors that have been shut on us. Society has made it seem as though things are impossible for us to achieve, but we will prevail, we will push through, we will be noticed, and we will be heard. Breaking down barriers and being heard will be our testament that we can persevere, not taking no for an answer. Imagine standing in front of a brick wall with no way around it unless you either climb it or turn around and give up. That thought of defeat can prevent you from making it through this hard wall. The wall represents your heartaches, disappointments, displeasures, moments of second-guessing yourself, and unbelief. I've learned that no matter what challenges lie ahead, I view them as already overcome. This winner's attitude, developed through hardships and heartaches, keeps me resilient. I draw from my inner strength to stabilize my thoughts, fighting and winning every time. My God-given stride grounds me in hope. Let this chapter be a hammer, breaking apart the obstacles in our lives. Speak to that one thing you struggle to overcome. Your faith and the words you speak over yourself will chip away at that wall, allowing you to cross over. Reimagine yourself, breaking free from delays to your season of promise. Freedom puts you in a mindset where you can do all things without feeling trapped. If we fail to communicate our ideas or desires, we hinder our own progress. A bad marriage or wrong friendships can be barriers. Toxic relationships often trap us in cycles of emotional turmoil and self doubt, draining our energy and distracting us from our goals. Emotional abuse, manipulation, and constant conflict lead to chronic stress and anxiety, affecting our mental and physical health. These relationships can isolate us from our support networks, deepening our sense of loneliness and helplessness and increasing isolation. Breaking free requires immense courage and a commitment to selflove and self-respect. Seeking support from loved ones, counseling, and self-help resources can provide the strength needed to navigate this journey. But ultimately, we have everything we need in ourselves; we were created perfectly in the image of God, and when we understand that truth, we are already halfway to where we need to be. By leaving detrimental relationships, we reclaim our peace and happiness, opening the door to a future filled with possibilities. Becoming "that girl" requires breaking down barriers for yourself, others, and your legacy. We must understand our true power. Our actions, whether positive or negative, affect the world around us. The barriers you break today impact your children and those close to you. There is a ripple effect every time we break a wall down, sometimes small and sometimes transformative. Taking bold stands at work or in your social life will have an impact. Being "that girl" means constantly evolving for the better. Breaking down barriers will be an everyday occurrence. Depression is a significant barrier that will keep you from having the energy to make things happen.

Depression is a barrier that will keep you in bed, isolated, unhappy, and hopeless. That girl is not hopeless; she is full of hope, and she constantly is renewing her mind and her spirit to take on the day and whatever may come with it, good or bad. Mental fortitude takes effort. You have to encourage yourself! You gotta make yourself get up and get it done. Women amaze me because I know firsthand how being a mother, having a career, a thriving business, and a social life can be draining if you allow it to be. Look at it from another perspective. Talk to yourself! Tell yourself you can do it. Tell yourself you are a winner and become one. Tell yourself you are amazing and do amazing things. No, it is not always going to be easy, but it is always going to be possible. When distractions come, speak to those things and break them down with your emotional and mental strength and capabilities. You are powerful! Your thoughts, words, and actions can accomplish so much if you allow them to. Have faith in yourself and keep going, no matter what the situation looks like. You have to know that you can make it through anything, and whether you continue to struggle through or dance through those moments is completely up to you and no one else. To be "That Girl"—the one who is unapologetically herself, who pursues her dreams with passion, and who inspires others to do the same—we must embody fearlessness. It's all about taking risks, speaking our truth, and loving ourselves fiercely. It's about breaking down barriers and helping others do the same. By living fearlessly, we transform our lives and create a world where women are empowered. Fearlessness and breaking barriers are inextricably linked.

One fuels the other, creating an unstoppable force within us. By embodying fearlessness, we develop the strength to break down barriers, unlocking our potential to live our best lives. We become "That Girl"–boldly striding through life, breaking barriers, and inspiring others. Together, let us live fearlessly, break down barriers, and create a world where being a woman is a powerful force for change. Let us dare to dream, act on those dreams, and forge our paths with unwavering determination and resolve.

UNAPOLOGETIC | UNSTOPPABLE

Chapter Four
Suicide

About seven years ago, my eldest son went through a very public suicidal situation. My son has always had a special calling on his life to be a voice for others. For most of his life, he has been dedicated to advocating for victims and the city of Chicago. He has made a name for himself by marching, protesting, and advocating against gun violence, police brutality, and injustices in our hometown. He is passionate and unapologetic in his delivery, a trait he inherited from me. He has always truly cared for our city and victims everywhere. Around this time, he had taken on a fight against our then-mayor, Rahm Emanuel. He was deeply committed to the fight and had given all of himself to the citizens of Chicago in many different forms. When he faced the tragic loss of a child he had taken under his wing as a son, he blamed himself. This young man, whom my son had sort of adopted, tragically took his own life. My son felt that, despite dedicating his fight, time, and life to advocating for Chicago, he had failed this young boy. He believed that if he had been there for him, the situation might have been different, and the boy wouldn't have ended his life. My son then hit a wall of desperation and despair. He began to hate himself and resented the city of Chicago and its citizens because he felt they didn't care about him after all the marches, cases, and fights. He felt abandoned by them and by the church as well. My son had also been a minister in his church for many years, another example of the great calling on his life that always compelled him to give to others, losing himself in the process. The sudden and tragic loss of this boy, whom my son loved with all his heart as if the child were truly his, was too much to bear. He couldn't handle the pain or the reality of the boy being gone. The possibility that he might have been able to save him if he had been more present consumed him. The grief and pain became overwhelming. We were sitting at the dinner table when we learned the news of this tragedy. I remember my son getting up from the table, and I stood up with him. We locked eyes, and the look in his eyes concerned me. I asked him, "Are you okay? "He nodded and said, "I'm about to go." In my God-given discernment, I knew something wasn't right. Two hours later, I received a call from a pastor friend close to our family. He informed me that my son had been on a livestream, holding a gun to himself. They had shut down Lake Shore Drive, and the police were trying to reason with him, begging him to come out of the car and put the weapon down. In the live stream, which I have never seen firsthand, he sobbed and stated repeatedly, "It's over." He explained how he blamed himself for the death of this young boy he loved. He was in complete despair and did not want to continue living. I know this might sound crazy to some, but when I got the call, I leaned into God's promises for my children. I felt no fear. Of course, I was saddened and concerned for my child, but I trusted God completely to provide my son with a way out. I immediately went into prayer. I couldn't drive to where the situation was taking place because they had shut down the road. So, I prayed and I prayed. I pressed into God's presence and I didn't move until God told me to. My son is alive and well today. He is successful, and happy, and has continued to make a name for himself by pursuing justice and accountability. I tell this story because there is a common theme with suicidal ideation and thoughts: desperation. The pain becomes so great that we can't see past it. We cannot see the escape that God always has for us because we are blinded by our own minds. Critical thinking goes out the window when something tragic or traumatic happens to us. It's like pain-filled blinders get put up, and unless someone is there to tell us and help us to get the blinders off, it seems as though the pain will not subside and will not end. So, who wants to live a life with that kind of pain? The never-ending kind, the kind that is so overwhelming that we just can't see how life will continue. It's like you're drowning in the middle of the ocean with not a soul, lifeboat, life vest, or land in sight. The saddest fact is that suicide is the number one cause of death. Think about that. There are so many ways that people can perish, and to know that the number one cause globally is when someone actually decides to take their life prematurely is absolutely heartbreaking. The fact that there are so many broken people and broken lives that so many hundreds and thousands of people make this choice is devastating. The fact that it's the number one cause, but it's also the most preventable just feels like there are so many wasted opportunities for these people. Suicide rates continue to increase due to their association with mental depression, which undermines our mental fortitude and leads us toward self-destruction. Many people contend with suicidal thoughts, often stemming from deeply embedded, unresolved issues triggered by past traumas. Despite the belief that suicide offers an escape from life's pressures, it's not a viable solution. Our adversary, exploiting our vulnerability, challenges our faith in God's ability to sustain us through adversity. It's fundamental to strengthen that mental fortitude and reach a point where we resist succumbing to this demonic strategy. Betrayal, failed relationships, rejection, abandonment, and depression are common triggers for suicidal ideation, reminding us of the importance of our mental health and strength. The constant renewal of our minds is needed to combat these intrusive and unhealthy thoughts. So many factors contribute to our susceptibility to depression and oppression. We have to recognize our worth and value. Bullying plays a major role in the prevalence of suicide and suicidal thoughts, especially among young people. That constant torment and degradation faced by those who are bullied can lead to feelings of worthlessness, isolation, and despair. Unrelenting pressure can push many people toward believing that ending their lives is the only escape from the pain. The correlation between bullying and suicide reminds us of the urgent need for interventions that address the root causes of bullying and provide support for those affected. Schools, communities, and families must work together to create environments where empathy and respect are prioritized and where victims of bullying can find refuge and support. I am reminded of different conversations I've had with women who were consumed with wanting to end their lives. Their suicidal thoughts overshadowed their ability to think differently. As I have listened, I always wanted to give them uplifting responses, ensuring they wouldn't feel judged or condemned. My response has been, "I totally get it and understand how you felt in that moment. But remember sis, it didn't prevail. You're sitting here, able to confide in me that this thing tried to take you out prematurely." I began to share my testimony of how it tried to defeat me as well. I believe strongly that our greatest weapon as women is sharing our similarities and differences. We must extend grace to ourselves. There was a time when my desperation reached a point where I also believed ending my life was the only way out. My heart was broken from trusting in people too much, and I never truly understood that deception or heartbreak could be such an impactful thing. I never knew how loving someone worked, and I was deeply infatuated with a man. I kept dreaming he wasn't right for me, but I didn't understand fully about my gift of knowing yet. After I caught him with the woman I had dreamt about—I saw him with her—I felt an overwhelming sense of betrayal. The feeling I had of wanting to hurt him turned into a desire to hurt myself instead. The day I caught him with her is forever etched in my memory. I remember the shock, the gut-wrenching pain, and that overwhelming sense of betrayal. The dream that had been haunting me suddenly made sense, and the truth was more painful than I could have imagined. My trust was shattered, and the pain was unbearable. I felt as though my entire world had collapsed around me. In that moment of profound sorrow, I made a desperate decision. I went to the bathroom, grabbed a bottle of painkillers, and swallowed them all. I remember the cold, sterile tiles of the bathroom floor as I sat there, the weight of my decision sinking in. I stumbled out of the bathroom, my vision blurring, and opened the door before collapsing onto the floor. My mom found me there, her face contorted in panic and fear. She rushed to my side, screaming my name, trying to keep me conscious. Through the fog, I could hear her asking if I had taken pills. I nodded yes, feeling the world slipping away from me. She called the ambulance, her voice trembling with fear and anguish. The ambulance arrived quickly, and the paramedics took over. They made me drink a black charcoal mixture to induce vomiting. The taste was awful, and the sensation of the charcoal going down my throat is something I will never forget. I vomited up the painkillers I had taken; each heave was a painful reminder of my desperate act. The paramedics then pumped my stomach to remove any remaining toxins. Throughout the entire process, my mom was by my side, asking over and over, "Why would you do this? What is going on?" I had no one to talk to and little knowledge of feelings, emotions, or relationship stuff. I was bait for Satan. After they stabilized me, I remember coming to my senses. No one is worth all this. My abandoned heart was ignored, so suicide became my go-to because the pain felt unescapable. Pain will lead you to a place of not loving yourself; it's a trap. The aftermath was a blur of hospital rooms, doctors, and nurses. The physical recovery was challenging, but the emotional recovery was even harder. I had to confront the pain and betrayal that had driven me to such an extreme. I had to learn to trust again and to open my heart to the possibility of healing and love. It was a long and difficult journey, but it was one I had to take. It seemed like the cycle repeated when I was faced with the situation involving my oldest son. Many years later, when he had his suicide attempt, I remember thinking about how our cycles just repeat and continue unless we make a bold stand. We must think differently; we must live differently. If you want to be different, you have to DO DIFFERENT THINGS! If your parents had/have struggles with addiction, you must then know that YOU and YOUR CHILDREN are susceptible to addiction. So, then you go on the offense and work against these things before they even form. We can't be "THAT girl" if we allow negatives to take over our minds. We need to take a second look at the cause and effect of our suffering and understand that it does not last as long as we might think. Although things may look hopeless, there always comes a season when you win. Always. We must believe it. Wallowing in despair only increases our misery; we need to change our thought patterns and think positively. Speaking positively is equally important—life and death are in the power of the tongue. The idea of being "THAT girl" who stands against suicide requires a bold rethinking of our attitudes and approaches toward mental health. To make a significant impact, we must challenge the stigmas surrounding mental illness and promote open conversations about feelings of despair and suicidal thoughts. Being "THAT girl" means advocating for mental health education, supporting friends and loved ones who are struggling, and encouraging others to seek help when needed. To truly embody the spirit of "THAT girl," we must stay focused and grounded in the belief that there is always a way out and that God provides us with the strength and resources to prevail. Your faith can be a source of immense comfort and guidance, offering a sense of purpose and direction when life feels overwhelming. Faith reminds us that we are not alone in our struggles and that there is a higher power invested in our well-being. By adopting a strong spiritual foundation and maintaining a connection to our faith, we can find the courage to face life's challenges and support others in their journey toward healing. Creative miracles happen when we elevate our thinking. The easy way out, suicide, is not a solution but a surrender to weaker forces. We must have a determination to live. An inner confession of "I wanna live" can be transformative. Even when we feel overwhelmed, hurt, and under pressure, drowning in misery, we must remember that nobody is beyond hope. Sometimes, the people around us whom we depend on are more wicked than we realize. It's vital to surround ourselves with strong, supportive people who can provide balance and encouragement. Even if you have had suicidal thoughts, it doesn't mean that you are weak. The strength within has only been smothered by grief and loss. We have to remember that it's all about mindset. Loss—whether of a loved one, a job, or financial stability—can be devastating, especially when those we relied on as crutches are no longer there. These struggles can trigger suicidal thoughts, but they don't define our strength or worth. God will always give us recompense. You just have to see past the immediate pain and trust in the possibility of a brighter future. By actively working to strengthen our mental and emotional health, we can overcome any challenge we face. Every life is precious, and each of us has the capacity to find hope and healing, even in the darkest of times. When we openly share our experiences and support each other, we create a community of strength and understanding. When we are open about our struggles, we offer a lifeline to those who might feel isolated and misunderstood. Our stories of survival can inspire others to hold on and seek help. We must face suicide head-on, making it a priority to address this issue cautiously. We must ensure that our loved ones know there is always a way out. As mothers, we need to be present and be good listeners for our kids, keeping the conversations going about what is troubling their souls. When our kids know they can talk to us about anything, we can help block the invasive thoughts of suicide from taking hold of their minds. We must also remember the importance of professional help. Therapy, counseling, and medication can provide amazing support and guidance. Please remember that seeking help is not a sign of weakness but a step towards healing and empowerment. Our mental health is a battlefield, and we must equip ourselves with the right tools and support to navigate it. Suicide has a way of drowning out the voice of reason, making it difficult for people to see beyond their immediate pain. The feelings of hopelessness and despair can become so overwhelming that they overshadow any rational thoughts or potential solutions. We must learn to recognize the signs of someone struggling and be willing to intervene with compassion and understanding. Being "that girl" is about more than just us personally; it is about becoming an advocate for change and a source of support for others. Through collective effort and unwavering faith, we can make a significant impact in the fight against suicide. I want to be clear here—suicide and suicidal tendencies are not limited to any one race or any one type of people. It reaches everyone. Everybody is susceptible to being in those darkest of places. Suicide is a significant public health issue affecting people from all walks of life. According to the World Health Organization, nearly 800,000 people die by suicide each year, making it a leading cause of death worldwide. Within a broader context, the African-American community faces unique challenges and higher risks regarding suicide. Historically, discussions about mental health have been stigmatized within many African-American communities and is often perceived as a sign of weakness or something to be handled privately. This cultural barrier to seeking help has severe implications. Statistics also reveal troubling trends: a study published showed that the suicide rate among African-American youth, particularly African-American boys aged 5-11, has been rising faster than in any other racial or ethnic group. The reluctance to discuss mental health issues can be traced back to deep-seated cultural norms and systemic factors. For many, expressing vulnerability is seen as a luxury they simply cannot afford, especially when dealing with the daily stressors of racism and economic hardship. This has created an environment where mental health issues are often unacknowledged and untreated. Women also face significant challenges regarding mental health and suicide. Women are more likely to experience certain mental health conditions, such as depression and anxiety, which are major risk factors for suicide. According to the American Foundation for Suicide Prevention (AFSP), while men are more likely to die by suicide, women are more likely to attempt suicide. This imbalance reflects the intense psychological burden many women typically carry. Women often juggle multiple roles—mothers, caregivers, professionals, and homemakers—leading to high levels of stress and emotional exhaustion. The expectation that women should seamlessly balance these responsibilities can create immense pressure. Many women, particularly mothers, feel they must prioritize their family's needs above their own, often neglecting their mental health in the process. There is a fear of shame there that should not be, and the belief that seeking help signifies weakness or inadequacy as a mother further discourages women from reaching out for support. Nearly one in five women in the United States experiences a mental health disorder, yet women are less likely to seek mental health care due to the perceived responsibilities associated with admitting they are struggling. This is especially pronounced in mothers who fear that acknowledging their struggles might impact their ability to care for their children and households effectively. Mental health professionals are increasingly recognizing the need for tailored approaches that address the unique challenges women encounter. As we move forward, it is absolutely critical to continue these conversations about the dark moments we experience in our lives. We should make sure that we do our part as human beings to ensure that everyone, regardless of race or gender, has the support and resources they need to overcome their darkest moments. What we need, now more than ever is a culture of openness and understanding. We can facilitate a future where mental health is prioritized and everyone feels empowered to seek help when they need it. Together, we can build a society that values mental well-being and supports everyone's journey toward healing and hope.

UNAPOLOGETIC | UNSTOPPABLE

Chapter Five
Intimidation & Manipulation

I know a girl with a powerful testimony; she has shared with me some of the traumatic experiences she has been through. She has gotten past all of those things and has become a very strong woman, mother, and wife despite all of the pain she experienced. I have her permission, and I want to share part of her story that has stood out to me as it relates to this chapter. When she was a kid, she was abused sexually by a boyfriend of a close family member of hers. This man preyed on her and manipulated her into these horrific sexual acts in secret. When she built up the courage to tell someone about what had happened, her family member found out and got angry with her, blaming her for what happened to her. This family member, in reality, was dating a very sick man, and now that I think about it in depth, all of the adults in this story had to be very sick, evil people. The girl was only 11 and he was an adult man. Now in the girl's young mind, she had been convinced by this man that what was happening was normal when two people 'liked' each other. He had spent a lot of time building up to what he did; he had been working on manipulating this young girl for a very long time. By little quiet compliments, 'playful' banter, inappropriately making faces and eye contact with her when no one was watching, stealing away a touch here or there that would look innocent to the naked eye or to adults around her who weren't really paying attention, or watching for anything inappropriate. The adults around who were supposed to be protecting her were so consumed in their own self-centered worlds that all of this flew under the radar for so long that it became (in her mind) regular and casual, even safe. The behavior grew more and more inappropriate, and the man grew more and more bold in his flirtations with her. Remember, she is a child surrounded by adults whose responsibility was to keep her safe and teach her about these kinds of things being dangerous, but nobody did. This was a 'long-game manipulation' for the man. He had ill intentions for the girl from the very beginning, but it was all masked by supposed innocent playfulness or teasing, and his real motives were hidden just enough to get away with. Women, we have to pay attention to who is paying attention to our children! We must watch closely EVERYTHING concerning our kids. There is evil in this world, and it is all around us, getting away with harming and hurting others; we just have to come out of our own headspace and pay close attention. When we don't, people get hurt and traumatized; we have to take care of each other! If you see something, say something! If you don't, who will? Anyway, after a long time of this insidious manipulation game with this young girl, this man took it to the next level and ended up sexually abusing her. Now think about your 11-year-old mind. Can you remember what you were like as an 11-year-old kid? Impressionable, easily manipulated, craving and needing attention, affection, and validation. A lot of times kids try and act or behave in ways that make them seem older; kids never want to be kids and enjoy their time as kids, steadily trying to be cool, and if they have older siblings, constantly trying to hang out with them and be like them and their friends. Really, an 11-year-old has no idea who they are; they are searching for their identities often in other people, wanting to be popular or liked by everyone because they think that will fulfill and sustain them. Especially an 11-year-old girl who nobody is truly watching or guarding; she was just falling through the cracks. Manipulators and abusers will watch and pay close attention to be able to pick a girl like she was out of a crowd. They have trained themselves to recognize anyone who will be manipulated and abused easily. So, this young girl was getting all of this attention from this older man and not being paid any mind by her parents or anyone else for that matter. This man convinced her through calculated, intricately tailored manipulation that they were 'in love' and that the abuse she suffered was what people that were in love did. She was so wound up by this man that he had actually made her believe there was nothing wrong with what he had done to her and what he had compelled her to do. This is how very important it is to pay attention to our children, and any loved ones for that matter. Anyone can be manipulated; don't think you are above this sort of manipulation because you are an adult. Adults are manipulated all the time into doing what they shouldn't and don't want to do. The man actually abused her on a road trip with her whole family in the van while he did it. The girl's father was driving, and every other seat in this van was occupied by the girl's family members. He did these unspeakable things to her over and over while her family sat there on this trip, completely unaware and oblivious. Manipulators will use their tools of deception on everyone around them. He had clearly manipulated everyone else too into thinking he wasn't a predator and that he was normal and safe to have around. She wasn't the only victim of the manipulation, just the one who paid the highest cost. After this trip, the girl ended up telling someone what happened, and she told them sort of excitingly like something 'good' had happened to her. Manipulators will hurt you and make you believe it was for your own good. This girl's head had been messed with so badly that she was confused when the adult she told was shocked and alarmed. She had no clue about the harm that had come to her and how it would affect her for the rest of her life and how all of her relationships would suffer in the future because of this thing that had happened. To make this story even worse, her relative, who was actually in a relationship with this man, when they found out they punished her, held her accountable, called her names, treated her terribly, alienated her, and abused her throughout the rest of her childhood and teenage years, even into early adulthood. Emotional manipulation is significant. Women are generally highly emotional beings and are susceptible to manipulation by emotion. This includes guilt-tripping, gaslighting, and playing the victim. Manipulators incite guilt to influence behavior, making you feel responsible for their misfortunes. Gaslighting makes you question your sanity, doubting your perceptions and reality. Manipulators may act hurt or play the victim when challenged, further confusing you. The young girl's relative began a long pattern of emotional manipulation and then intimidation on this girl, and when the young girl was 15, her relative manipulated her into taking methamphetamine for the first time, and the girl became addicted and completely dependent on the drug and that relative to provide it for her. Again, using the fact that this young girl was clearly broken and felt guilty about what happened to her, she blamed herself for being abused and carried the fault and responsibility all on her own to ultimately attempt to ruin the young girl's life. Psychological manipulation uses mind games. This person played a never-ending mind game manipulation on the girl, and she never even realized she was being played with since she trusted this family member. It never even registered until many years later that she was controlled and used by these people. This person wanted to punish the young girl so badly that she devised a plan to get the young girl addicted to drugs and manipulate her need for that drug to use the young girl and eventually discard her when done utilizing her for her own benefit and entertainment. The young girl was made to be locked in a room for days at a time to babysit kids that weren't even hers so that the relative could move freely and party without having to worry about watching her own children. The young girl missed so much school she was held back, had to go to continuation school, and ended up becoming a runaway when the person providing her with drugs discarded her. But not before introducing her to another adult man who would manipulate and give the young girl a false sense of safety and accompany her while on the run; this man, who was knowingly with a teenage girl, also manipulated her and at first created a soul tie with her through sex. This was the girl's first sexual relationship, and it was with a grown adult man who knew just how to use a life of sex, drugs, and freedom from parental rules on a teenage girl. She was on drugs, away from home, and had only him to depend on and look to for everything, which was right where he wanted her. He used that sexual relationship to manipulate her into thinking she was safe with him and that he would protect her and love her in a way no one ever had, including her parents and family. He often told her how he could never hurt her and that he would always protect her from anyone who would. He repeatedly would explain how if he ever laid a hand on her, his family would disown him. For the first few months while they were on the run together, he was working overtime to convince her that he was a good guy. Pay close attention to people who feel they need to 'convince' you of things about themselves. You know, those people who, every chance they get, talk at great length about themselves and all their amazing qualities, all of the things they are good at, the things they know how to do well, that no one else can do as well as them. This is a form of manipulation. People with actual confidence, skill, and ability do not spend so much time talking about it. Those people who have a story for everything—they have had every job, been every place, done everything—they are trying to overcompensate for something, and it is usually a strategy used to relate to you in some way so that you let your guard down. That's what she did—she let her guard down, and right when she did, he pounced on the opportunity to assert control and dominance. She said or did something that apparently made him angry, and he hit her. Slapped her right across her face, so hard that her ears rang. She had never been abused in that way before; her parents never hit her across the face. Now this man had used sex and alienation from her parents to gain access to her completely. She had let him into her mind, her heart, and her body. She was shocked and confused and began to cry. When he noticed her tears, he turned on the waterworks as well, crying and apologizing, pretending as if he were ashamed of himself. He began to beg and plead with her to forgive him and swore he would never do anything like that ever again, like he couldn't believe that had happened. As if it just 'happened'. Another manipulation strategy. At this point, the girl has been away from her family for months; she was strung out on drugs, had no money, and only ate food every so often when he provided it for her. He had trapped her in a situation where she felt there was no escape, and she had become completely dependent on him for everything. Coercive manipulation uses threats, isolation, and economic control. Food, drugs, protection, sex because she had become addicted to that as well, and how it made her feel. She was now scared of the guy but didn't feel like she could just leave and go home; she was afraid of being in trouble for being a runaway for so long; she was trapped. Every single day after that one, she was beaten and hit repeatedly, thrown across rooms and parking lots like she wasn't a person but a trash bag that had no weight or significance. Intimidation was used every single day to keep her there with him, as a punching bag. You see, intimidation frequently works hand-in-hand with manipulation; both are toxic forms of control. He made her believe her family didn't care about her and that they didn't want her home anyway, and when she got desperate enough to say she didn't care about what her family would do or what kind of trouble she would be in, he threatened to actually kill her if she left him. He put a knife to her throat and told her if she tried to go home, he would end her life. Intimidation includes physical threats, stalking, and violence; verbal bullying, shouting, and ultimatums; social humiliation, rumors, exclusion, psychological mind games, fear mongering, and authority abuse. This went on for months until the girl was finally rescued. Someone called her parents and told them where she was; they came and picked her up and took her away to a completely different city far away so she could get away from all of the things, including him, that had her so bound. The damage was done, though. After all she endured, she continued to live a life of chaos and suffered much more abuse. She was addicted to drugs for almost 20 years of her life and continued to be manipulated and abused emotionally by that family member from the beginning of the story–the one who blamed her and persecuted her when she was supposed to actually protect her. Until she had enough. She had enough of being abused and manipulated and changed her life, and after all of it registered and she truly understood what had happened to her from a young age, she relieved herself of that guilt, and now that she, being an adult, understood that she was in fact manipulated and abused and taken advantage of and not protected by the people who were supposed to, she began to release all of those things one at a time. It didn't happen overnight; it was long and still is a work in progress. There is so much to process and heal from, but she became committed to becoming the woman that she was meant to be and the person who was almost stolen from her. She lived in torment for many, many years that the man would find her and hurt or kill her; she was paralyzed with fear for a very long time. Manipulation and intimidation, often subtle and always insidious, are tactics used to control others' thoughts, emotions, and behaviors. I told this story because I need you to understand the ramifications of manipulation and intimidation. They are literally strategies used by evil people to hurt us and keep us under their control. Lives can be ruined, and people can be seriously damaged when these tools are used to control. These strategies exploit vulnerabilities to achieve the manipulator's goals, hiding in misery, rejection, and insecurity, waiting to strike. We must identify when manipulation is used as a weapon against us and learn to protect ourselves and push back. As women, we must train ourselves to recognize and resist these tactics, which can feel like a form of sorcery against us. If we don't stay vigilant in our relationships and anticipate these maneuvers, we risk heartbreak and the destruction of our peace and happiness. We also risk our physical and emotional well-being. Falling prey to manipulation and intimidation endangers not only our own well-being but also that of our children, family, and loved ones. The girl is now a woman, and she is a testament to strength and determination. She uses what she has been through to help liberate others. She is the mother/parent/sister/family/ protector she needed when she was young and left completely open for those people to attack. That young girl is now THAT girl, facing every trial and struggle with an amazing ability to face the world and all its ugliness with courage and still loving openly without apprehension, with her head held high. She wears it all so well, you would never know unless she told you what she has been through because she still treats everyone with kindness, respect, and dignity. The evil she experienced in this world has not made her bitter or resentful. If anything, it has helped her show more compassion. The reason I absolutely felt an obligation to share her story is that all of us have a story that needs to be told. The world needs to hear how you prevailed through the trials of your life. Somebody, somewhere, is waiting to hear a testimony that they can relate to in order to find the right escape for them. We must tell our story, holding back nothing. Manipulation is often used as warfare in battles we may not even realize we're fighting. Some people choose deception over honesty, playing games with others' lives instead of focusing on themselves. Every life matters greatly, and we waste time and energy on these negative behaviors. It all boils down to control. Some people spend their lives trying to control everything, including others' lives. While we do control our own behavior and decisions, God is the ultimate authority; we should release control and allow only God to take over. Under no circumstances should we try to change or control anyone else. It's time to reclaim our lives and stop allowing people and things to control us. Control can consume us, taking away our ability to think for ourselves. Recognizing these behaviors helps us protect ourselves. Be wary of manipulation through silence, where someone plots against you quietly, studying your weaknesses to strike. This can come from those closest to us, disguised as concern or advice. Trust your instincts; a woman's intuition is powerful and often truthful. If something doesn't feel right, it usually isn't. Projection and triangulation are other forms of psychological manipulation. Projection is when the manipulator accuses you of their own dishonest behavior. Triangulation introduces a third party to distract, divide, and conquer through manipulation. This one is extra devious; it's like a group effort to control and hurt someone. Narcissistic manipulation includes love bombing, silent treatment, and blame-shifting. Women, we must train our discerning spirit. We need skilled, discerning minds, knowing when to speak and when to stay silent. Watch out for gift-giver manipulation, love bombing, and flattery manipulation. Manipulators may want you to conform because they are threatened by your uniqueness. Be wary of ulterior motives and manipulation through sex, which can create soul ties. Remember, sex does not equal love. Lust can disguise itself as love, but it is fleeting, while real love is unconditional and eternal. Do not use your body to get what you want; be a woman of substance, knowing your worth beyond physical appearance. Relationships are challenging enough without adding manipulation. Manipulation can trap you in a cycle of deceit, designed to destroy and keep us stuck in harmful patterns. The enemy will use our past against us in relationships, causing repeated cycles. Learn from past wounds to grow and elevate, not to reopen them. In the workplace, intimidation may come from those who think they are worth more because they earn more. Cliques manipulate and intimidate through a false sense of belonging, making you an outcast. Sometimes women will try to intimidate other women with material things. Acting like they are better than you because they have designer bags, look down on you and try to make you feel less than them, diminish your confidence, and attempt to violate your self-esteem. It is a mind-control mechanism to make themselves feel superior and better about themselves than they actually do in reality. Only insecure women use these kinds of intimidations; do not fall for it. Be secure in yourself and who you are in God's eyes. When you know courage, it is difficult to be intimidated. Bullies target those they perceive as weak. Stand up for yourself; be strong and courageous, as the Bible says. Don't be intimidated by insecure and weak individuals. We got to set boundaries, seek support, and practice assertiveness. Awareness is the first step to combating manipulation and intimidation. Assertiveness is the second. Recognize the signs and understand when someone is trying to manipulate you. Set clear boundaries and do not allow others to cross them. Build your self-confidence, as manipulators prey on those with low self-esteem. Know your worth and stand tall in your value. Surround yourself with supportive people. A strong support system helps you see through manipulation and provides strength to stand firm. Lean on your faith. Remember biblical truths that empower you to reject fear and embrace the power, love, and sound mind God has given you. The Bible offers wisdom on dealing with intimidation and manipulation. Manipulation and intimidation are yokes of bondage, and we must stand firm against them, asserting our freedom in Jesus. Trusting in the Lord is our ultimate defense against those who seek to intimidate or manipulate us. We are not called to live afraid or under others' control but in the freedom and authority given by God. As we navigate our lives, let us do so with confidence, knowing we are strong, capable, and free from manipulation and intimidation. It's time to reclaim our lives, assert our freedom, and live as the powerful women we are meant to be. Together, we can crush the heads of serpents designed to defeat us, knowing no defeat because we are "THAT GIRL." Let's stand firm, resist manipulation and intimidation, and inspire other women to do the same. Our lives, our responses, and our freedom matter greatly. Let's live in that truth and walk boldly into our destiny.

Chapter Six

Competitive Jealousy

Why do we, as women, often find ourselves competing with other women? This competition, fueled by jealousy, is a mindset that women of all ages, races, and backgrounds participate in and operate from on an everyday basis. It's behavior that has not only been normalized but has also actually become the norm. I have seen many things centered around competitiveness and jealousy. For example, I have seen mothers competing with their daughters and daughters competing with their mothers. Mother-in-law and daughter-in-law, Father and sons, and sons and fathers. Competing for love and acceptance, competing for attention, competing work ethic, competing literally to no end. What I have realized is that so many people are consumed with jealousy and competitive nature, and it has become a part of who they are. Let's remember that the atmosphere and situations we are born into have so much influence on who we become as adults. Meaning that if you are born of an unhealthy, distorted union, that will become your first and ultimate example of what marriages and unions are supposed to be like, but that is simply false. Let's start there. Our origin and upbringing will always have a lasting impact on who we become. I used to not be able to wrap my mind around seeing mothers and daughters, fathers and sons, in constant competition with each other. Being jealous of one another. My assistant and I were speaking about this today as a matter of fact. She was explaining to me how she and her husband never had an example of a solid marriage at home growing up. Her husband's father was murdered when he was very young, and because of that trauma, his mother checked out and got wrapped up in drug addiction and all that comes with that lifestyle, so she was absent, and dad was gone, so he ended up having to grow up very quickly and ended up having to assume the role of mother and father for his sister. Without him, they wouldn't have been able to eat a lot of times. Without having loving, responsible parents, he got lost in trying to be a man at 9 years old. He never really got to be a kid, and he certainly never had an example of a loving, fruitful marriage. Her parents, on the other hand, were married, and in her eyes, they were the perfect pair. She never witnessed any fights or anything that would make her think otherwise until one day when she came home to her mom gone and her dad explaining that their marriage was over, which completely shocked her because she was so young, she didn't understand 'grown-up' problems, so they hid those problems from her, and then all of a sudden one day it was over and everything was different. Mom was gone, and dad was responsible for everything at that point. So, when these two kids grew up and eventually found each other and decided to get married after the initial newness wore off and the honeymoon phase was over, they realized that they had no idea how to be married or what that even entailed or looked like because they lacked that example early on. They had to figure out all of this on their own, with no actual lead to follow and nobody to teach them anything about a godly union and marriage; they had to mold themselves! This is what I have had to come to understand about people and what makes them do what they do and become what they become. It has so much to do with the upbringing. You simply cannot follow what you have never seen. Everything we see and experience when growing up sets the stage for the rest of our lives. Sometimes we have to mold ourselves into what we know to be true and right. Or even what we learn to be correct and true later in life. It is different for everyone, but there will always come a point in your life where you will have to decide who you are going to be, in spite of who you might have been raised to be. In terms of not being able to wrap my head around the competitive jealousy that parents exhibit toward their children and the other way around, I had to fully understand that it almost always begins with that upbringing. When a mother is jealous of her daughter and in competition with her, more than likely she learned that from her mother first. This thing is generational! This is why it is so important to break those generational curses and habits as soon as possible because they will just keep going and going. Society and women seem to be completely oblivious to the fact that so many of us operate from a competitive place, and we are so broken that we do not even realize that we are in fact behaving, thinking, and speaking in a way that is dangerous and can become hurtful and lead to malice. Competitiveness and jealousy go hand in hand, and jealousy regularly leads to some form of cruelty. Not only will those two lead to exhibiting viciousness and being mean to the actual people you are jealous of and in competition with, but in the end will lead you to live a truly miserable life. So, ladies, let me bring this discussion to you and sit this on your lap. Competitiveness and jealousy among women has become like a cancer, eating away at us. Being competitive is like running a marathon with no finish line. It is never-ending. Someone will always seem to be better than you or look better than you. have more money than you and be smarter than you if your mindset is competition and jealousy. Competitiveness is also much like a deadly game that can cause great pain to yourself and to others as well if you get stuck in that way of thinking. That mindset will alter the way you behave and can make you disrespectful toward other women, all stemming from jealousy. Then your motives become questionable. That behavior is not only exhausting but also damaging to our well-being. I decided to add this chapter because I see this kind of thing happening so frequently: women being unable to come together to get anything of value done because we are stuck in these destructive patterns of competitive jealousy. More often than not, you will come across women who refuse to befriend other women because they have either been the target of competitiveness and jealousy or they have it in themselves. Women will use the excuse "I just don't get along with other women." Or "Most of my friends are men, women are mean, and I just get along with men more." Both of those are cop-outs. We are not called to run with the men; we are called to uplift and collaborate with other women; we just refuse to do the work that is required to break down those walls that prevent us from getting close to other women. It's as if we are unwilling to take the time to self-reflect and figure out why this behavior is constantly displayed. Yes, the WHY is always very important. Many times, competitive behaviors stem from deep-seated insecurities. Daily, we are reminded of the fact that we are not happy with who we are. That is the source of it all. Undeniably, the very core of a competitive, jealous spirit comes from not being secure in yourself and not having self-esteem. There are so many contributing factors when it comes to why we do or do not love ourselves. Trauma, relationship trauma, family trauma, etc. If you had parents that abandoned you, or if you were abused as a child, those very real and unfortunate events have a real lasting impact on who you become as an adult. We have to be mindful and look inward if we are to correct our behavior and thought patterns. Those deep-seated insecurities will lead to baseless fears and doubts, especially in relationships. It can also lead to trying to imitate or compete with other women in various aspects of life, like appearances, possessions, or relationships. When we are wrestling with competitiveness, we will see ourselves as unattractive and unhappy and constantly compare ourselves to others. That mindset of comparison causes us to be competitive. Competing with another woman means slowly losing your own identity. It smothers your self-esteem and leads to overcompensation for attention from others. When we feel the need to compete, it's because of a lack of self-confidence and an inability to embrace our own uniqueness. And get this: competition is often us struggling, fighting, or warring with someone else who doesn't even know you are fighting with them. It will always produce more self-doubt, more insecurities, and the need for more validation. Can't we see that, as women, it's a ploy to keep us from being unified? It's taking away from us being a strength to our sisters, mothers, daughters, friends, colleagues, and any women we may deal with on a day-to-day basis. I know for myself that I have endured a lot of sorrow throughout my life because I have always given my all to others to help them become and see the best version of themselves; in fact, I have committed the better part of my life to women to help them in the betterment of themselves. I have mentored, counseled, and worked with all kinds of women. What I have experienced is so much jealousy and women constantly competing with me from every angle. Many times, I have been working with women who were completely consumed with this overachiever mindset and attitude that in reality came purely from jealousy and a competitive nature toward me. If I had an idea, they had to come up with an even better one. Always needing to one-up someone. I have truly seen this and dealt with this in every environment. They feel like they need to measure up or prove something to someone that has minimized them or made them feel like they are incompetent, somewhere in their past, but will take it out on everyone else. I have dealt with this even with women that were on my team. Having to always be self-satisfying, and usually what they were doing wasn't bringing any satisfaction to others because it came from a place that wasn't genuine. I have looked through the window of their intentions, and they were not pure. People will compete with my insight and that something special that is inside of me. Because I have this gift, people are often intimidated by me and that gift. When people find out what's inside of me, they get jealous. They always want that profound wisdom to come from them because they feed on the attention and praise from people that they think belong to them and no one else. I had to make a decision for myself a long time ago to fight vigorously against the demonic activity that tries to tear me down, and I had to choose to separate myself. I look to God because he is the one who made me and gave me these gifts and attributes. I've had to resist the urge to let flesh overtake me and fight carnally for myself against these things. I constantly look to Him, and he handles my problems and fights my battles for me. I cannot help that I am THAT girl, truly. I was chosen, and I simply can't help that. I have had to stay separated from a lot of people; I walk alone mostly, yet not alone. And I am okay with that. It has been quite rewarding to commit to not allowing any negativity to invade my space. My difference is DIFFERENT. God has repeatedly proven himself in my life; he is with me fully and wholly, and I do not need validation from man whatsoever. I compete with no one. As a woman who says this all the time, "I'm every woman," I know my identity, and I have confidence in who I am. I simply don't know how to compete with another woman. I'm just not that girl. That space is a dangerous one. Sometimes we even compete with the unknown because we are so delusional and assume things are a certain way and they just are not. While we are wasting time competing, others are reaching milestones in their lives and getting themselves to the finish line. Women who do not spend time thinking about what another woman is doing or how they look are busy making something of themselves. They are meeting goals. Celebrating wins, etc. Being consumed with the lives of other women is such wasted time, talent, and energy. We want to look like someone else instead of enhancing what we have. Sometimes, being our original selves is painful. It's time to break free from this cycle. We need to work on ourselves. We should invest in ourselves rather than trying to become someone else. We need to reconsider our actions and relationships to avoid being consumed by competitive jealousy. We have to be mindful of the company we keep and be wary of competitive tendencies. It's important to watch out for coveting what others have, as it is a destructive path. We gotta move away from competition, as it is not our friend. This behavior takes away from being our sister's keeper and prevents unity among women. It's time to redefine ourselves and take the time to uplift one another. Competing with other women takes you further and further away from knowing your true self. We need to spend time with ourselves and refrain from comparing and competing with others. Every woman is on her own journey, and we all have unique strengths and weaknesses. Instead of viewing and treating other women as competition, we should view them and treat them as allies. It's important to learn from each other, support each other, and grow together. Jealousy is a natural emotion, but it's important to have self-awareness of this stronghold and use that awareness as motivation to improve ourselves. We must focus on our individual growth and learn to celebrate our own achievements. The Bible addresses jealousy in various passages, cautioning believers against harboring this destructive emotion. Scriptures about jealousy emphasize the importance of contentment and trust in

God's providence, discouraging the poisonous effects of jealousy on relationships and spiritual well-being. For instance, in Proverbs it says, "A tranquil heart gives life to the flesh, but envy makes the bones rot." This verse highlights the destructive nature of jealousy. Also, James says, "For where jealousy and selfish ambition exist, there will be disorder and every vile practice." This verse warns us of the chaos and negativity that jealousy can bring into our lives. We should have the mindset and a heartfelt desire to see every woman win and not interfere with their personal growth or their lives because of our own insecurities. I strongly believe that the things we operate from often put down roots in our struggles. Why keep allowing ourselves to operate in these mannerisms? Girl, it's not that serious. When we compete with others, we're not acknowledging our individuality. Instead, we're comparing our behind-the-scenes with someone else's highlight reel. Remember, there's enough room for every woman to succeed. The success of one woman doesn't diminish the success of another. To overcome competitiveness and jealousy, we need to fully understand what truly lies beneath these feelings. It's important to focus on the positives in our lives, support and uplift other women, set personal goals aligned with our values, learn from others, and replace negative thoughts with positive affirmations. Competitiveness and jealousy are challenges many women face, but they are not insurmountable. We must figure out how to prevent this jealousy and competitiveness from consuming our identity. We also need to understand that competitiveness will spill over to our love affairs as well, preventing us from showing up as someone different and not ourselves. We will show up as incomplete. We will compete with the man in the bedroom, through sex, through conversation, and with getting things done in your home. We have this preconceived notion that competing with our significant other is ok and it is not. You are just wasting time trying to show up as someone you simply are not, even in front of our men. Have we ever taken note that our churches are filled with women? Women are doing the homework with the kids, women are in the school pickup lines, women are at the grocery store, making dinner and then doing the dishes and laundry–all of it! We tend to blame the men for these things, but we are in actuality the problem. We cannot seem to let go of this need to control and be better at everything. It is a behavior disorder. A lot of relationships have been perverted and are unbalanced because we have decapitated the 'head of household'. We have unfruitful unions because we have put our husbands in a chokehold, taking away their ability and their calling to lead in the home. We insist on doing everything better ourselves, and in doing so, we remove the need for a man in the home. Letting him lead you and the rest of your household is the way God intended, yet we refuse to give up any control in any aspect. We complain the house is dirty but will not allow anyone else to clean it because we believe we are the only ones that will do it correctly. We insist on making all the decisions for our household. We have this need to make more money and have a better job, just staying in constant competition with the person who is supposed to be our partner and the actual head of our home. We create an environment where our children only want and depend on 'Mommy' for everything. We have made the men in our lives insecure by this incessant need to control everything and be better at everything. Then we get upset and complain to others about having to do it all by ourselves. Competitive jealousy is that thing that will infiltrate every single area of your life until it is full of chaos and disarray. We have to work actively against adopting these traits before they completely ruin us. In the grand scheme of things, it's important to remember that every woman is on her own journey. Each of us is unique, with our own strengths, weaknesses, dreams, and fears. By embracing our individuality, supporting one another, and seeking guidance from our faith, we can overcome these destructive behaviors. The journey to self-acceptance and inner peace is ongoing, but with each step, we grow stronger, more confident, and more united. As women, let us strive to uplift one another and create a world where every woman can shine in her own light. Being a copycat or a person who is trying to be like someone else or better than them may appear to be an easier way to live, but only because it is all you are used to. If you find yourself feeling jealous of another woman's success, ask yourself why. What is it about her success that triggers these feelings in you? Once you've identified what the real cause is, only then can you work on addressing it. Remember that confidence comes from within. It's not about being better than someone else; it's about being the best version of yourself. Focus on your own growth and development.

Celebrate your achievements, no matter how small they may seem. And most importantly, love yourself. Because at the end of the day, you're not just any girl you're THAT GIRL. The girl who is confident, strong, and unapologetically herself. Find yourself; redefine yourself. You can take as long as you need to become the woman you want to be, but choose to be the woman who always uplifts and never tears down. The only thing we should be doing is spreading positivity from one woman to another. We should not be trying to clone other women or compete with them. We have to realize that doing things of that nature takes you further and further away from knowing your true self. Make a conscious effort to support and uplift other women. Celebrate their successes and be genuinely happy for their achievements. Start now and smile at her efforts, her accomplishments, and her uniqueness. Let the other woman be herself; stop trying to control her life by making it your own. Why try and take something that doesn't belong to you, like another woman's identity? Get your own. The best way to start that is by getting to know you. Spend time with yourself. Don't fill up the time that you have with comparing and competing with others. Take time to reflect on your emotions and then begin to unearth the very foundational cause of your competitiveness and jealousy. Understanding why you feel this way is the first step towards change. Focus on the positives in your life. Keep a gratitude journal and regularly write down things you are thankful for. This helps shift your focus from what you lack to what you have. Set personal goals that align with your values and passions. Focus on your own journey and measure your progress against your past self, not against others. Look to other women for inspiration, not as benchmarks to measure your worth. Learn from their journeys and apply those lessons to your own life. Replace negative, comparative thoughts with positive and uplifting thoughts. Remind yourself of your unique qualities and strengths. To be THAT girl is to love yourself fully and completely while actively building other women up and helping them find themselves and fall in love with who they are. THAT girl is always looking for ways to assist other ladies in becoming THAT girl too. THAT girl is not a gatekeeper; she wants to be surrounded by strong, caring, kind, positive, confident, and powerful women, so she does everything she can to help them achieve that position. Competitive jealousy simply does not exist in THAT girl's circle because she extinguishes those negative feelings that her friends and loved ones have for themselves and others.

Chapter Seven

Women In Leadership

I decided to write about women leaders in this chapter to serve as an example of hope and encouragement for all of us and to shed light on the very essence of our being. We, as women leaders, are often kept in a box. Many times, people try to mishandle us and keep us from our seat at the table, but I am starting to see that we are overcoming many obstacles and becoming "THAT Girl," who will fight vigorously to ensure our place in society is no longer overlooked. This struggle reminds me of the story of Adam and Eve in the Garden of Eden. God created Adam and placed him in the Garden of Eden to take care of it. Later, God created Eve from Adam's rib to be his companion. They had the freedom to eat from any tree in the garden except for one—the tree of the knowledge of good and evil. This tree was off-limits, and God warned that eating its fruit would lead to death. Eve's encounter with the serpent and her decision to eat the forbidden fruit is a pivotal moment. Eating the fruit, despite the prohibition, symbolizes a quest for knowledge and autonomy, but it also brings about significant consequences. The idea of being "forbidden" resonates deeply with many women's experiences throughout history and even today. Just like Eve was forbidden to eat the fruit, many women have historically been discouraged from speaking out. Societal and cultural expectations often silence women's voices, making it tough for them to express their thoughts and opinions freely. Let me have this conversation with you. What makes a good leader? What constitutes effective leadership? Our mindset is vitally important. We must ensure our thoughts are geared toward positivity in all regards. Having respect, communication, accountability, and leading by example is important. Let's talk a bit about the mindset that is required for leadership. A lot of times, leaders underestimate the value of having a made-up mind. The Bible says a double-minded man is unstable in all his ways; let's be clear, that means all mankind, women included. You can change it up if it will help you really understand how important this is. "A double-minded WOMAN is unstable in all HER ways." It all starts with your made-up mind. All of it. Leadership: most of all, double-mindedness in leadership can be incredibly detrimental. When a leader is duplicitous, they send mixed signals to their team, creating confusion and mistrust. That kind of inconsistency can undermine the leader's credibility and make it difficult for team members to follow their direction confidently. When leaders are not consistent in their decisions and actions, it becomes challenging for team members to trust them. Trust is foundational in any leadership role, and without it, a leader's effectiveness is severely compromised. Double-mindedness leads to uncertainty and indecision. Teams need clear, decisive leadership to navigate challenges and achieve goals. A leader who wavers can cause delays and missed opportunities. Now, this thing works both ways, it has to be an exchange. Let's be clear, team members also have a responsibility to check their baggage to follow effectively. You cannot expect to function on a high level workable team if you bring discontentment and strife to your leader or your team as a whole. To lead effectively, a leader must have a clear and unwavering vision. Clarity, consistency, and confidence are vital to anyone in leadership, but women most of all because there is this stigma that surrounds women that we are emotional and operate from an emotional standpoint rather than an intelligent one. We can do both, by the way. I feel we are so powerful because we can use our emotional strength as well as intellect to guide and help us make the right decisions. It is not a weakness to open our hearts and lead from there; it is a strength to use both heart and mind; that is what makes us so powerful and strong, but we are so often looked down upon for using our hearts, so we tend to view that as a downfall rather than a strength, and that is a mistake. Good leaders possess a level of expertise that is unmatched. We inspire others to become the best version of themselves by leading them down a path of success in leadership. Our core values, which we set for ourselves, will sustain us when we fully understand our WHY in leadership. What makes a good leader in us women is the ability to be steadfast, focused, vigilant, and strong. We have wit, wisdom, creativity, and poise, and we will remain steadfast in our mindset of triumph. No matter what we face, we will make it; we will overcome. These qualities are necessary, but there are many more that contribute to effective leadership. As a leader, I have learned that I must continuously embrace these qualities because ultimately effectiveness is my goal. What I have come to realize is there are two types of leaders: you can be born a leader or rely on man to make a leader out of you. I am a born leader, which comes with the highest level of maturity and a discerning spirit, knowing your true identity. It is also vitally important to have a clear path, always moving in the right direction. You gotta know that you know! Being a born leader requires me to be a staple that holds things together. Man-made leaders are usually those with degrees. They tend to have an arrogance about them. Because of their degree, they feel they have leadership unlocked. But I feel we need to pay attention to the similarities and the differences. Let me give it to you just like this: the similarity is we both have trauma responses; we're similar in having anxiety issues; we still have to study to show ourselves approved; we are still challenged in areas of mental stability; and we must maintain emotional security. We still have to cultivate our potential and unlock it. And let's not forget determination. More than anything, no matter what kind of leader you are or aspire to be, we should share the same sentiment in learning how to follow first. Our differences are that just having book knowledge (from schooling) does not make you more qualified without having some level of spirituality intertwined that will make you better equipped to lead. You have to be personable, have grace, and know how to go in and out amongst all types of people. You have to have empathy and compassion; you have to be able to meet people where they're at. We must be careful not to be overly critical and judgmental of others aspiring to lead. We can kill their spirit and their desire or drive to lead by being overly harsh. We should never be indifferent and should always lead with love. Sometimes love comes in the form of correction, but we must be careful in our delivery of that correction so that we are not too harsh. We must lead with grace and understanding. To all women born to lead, I say,

"Let's be the best version of ourselves and show up right, no matter the opposition we face or any pushback that may occur." We should make our footprint readable and easy to follow by being consistent in walking toward fulfilling our destiny. Being born a leader means we operate from a level of understanding that is unmatched. Leaders have the ability to articulate, communicate, and understand with their hearts, possessing an in-depth insight. Women, let's boldly declare our position with the right attitude toward those we are entrusted to lead. True leaders are unbothered by attacks and vile speech against them. Because they are leaders, they are more susceptible to these attacks yet remain unbothered and strong. Being a leader requires self-denial in many spaces and providing the best possible solutions to create peace and stability around us. I have learned that the things that have bothered me or made me feel uncomfortable are the things that God graced me with to challenge me to change. I have also had to confront many issues head-on. I knew that people would either draw closer to me or run away. Being a woman who speaks the truth will not always be received well, and I am okay with that because they did the same to the example I follow—God. No one can deny His existence. Let me also touch on this: if you are actively contributing to the division of someone else's household, have you considered that it will be your household that will remain that way? Let me explain. I have witnessed many times women will prey on another woman's happiness or marriage because of jealousy or insecurity, and in the end, it is their household that will ultimately pay the price. I have even seen this with women in church leadership. Some people are just in it for the wrong reasons; they have a need to control or a desire for power that will lead them to literally work behind the scenes to destroy others' lives. By manipulation and other evil tactics. The way God speaks to me and through discernment, I do not have to know your story to tell the truth. I am gainfully employed. because I work for GOD. We have to always be wary of folks who will use their position for negative works. We have to hold ourselves accountable and make sure we hold our leaders accountable as well. When you are in a leadership role where you have people who depend on you and trust you to have their best interests in mind, you have to check the condition of your heart. Are your intentions pure? What are your intentions? What is your motivation? We as leaders hold people's lives in our hands, and we have to do right by them. It has to be from a loving place and a place of genuine care and concern. Otherwise, we just cause more harm than anything, and chaos erupts in others' lives, and when you sew chaos, that is exactly what you will reap in your own. We, as women leaders, should have the courage to lead with self-awareness, integrity, and mindfulness of others. We should never blindly lead, we have to know them that labor amongst us. I have guided many women in the right direction in their lives, cultivating what is already inside them—things they did not even see in themselves yet. I have spoken to business owners who could not envision a strategy for growth, and I have seen the end results looking simply amazing. My encouragement to them is an echo of my own confidence in knowing. When I reflect on the tests of time that I have endured, I remember being mislabeled, misunderstood, and even talked about. These experiences only further developed me into the woman I am today–the one who does not allow the opinions of others to deter me from providing a quality of leadership that stands out. I have helped others soar, discover their identity, face their fears, and become whole. I have provided hope and taught them to persevere through faith, recognizing that their God-given potential has no limits. I helped them realize that being relentless will always keep them standing and moving forward. Yeah, I'm THAT girl. In my leadership as a mentor, I have the tools that include impeccable social skills, inner motivation, and knowing balance for fruitful living. Speaking to the entrepreneur or business owner, let me encourage you! I am a serial entrepreneur who knows what having a thriving business can look like. I've owned restaurants and beauty salons, where I have employed over 20 people at one time. I kept the momentum in excellence, always having a readiness in my heart to reach the finish line in servitude. I was my own wind at my back, pushing myself forward because of what has been embedded in me as a born leader. I stayed in constant communication with myself, keeping me a step ahead and always anticipating the next big move. I stayed in constant communication with myself but always listened for that small, still voice, unfolding new strategies to build. In entrepreneurship, I just want to give you a brief synopsis on the steps to take in starting your business. When thinking about entrepreneurship, it's important to consider how social media can benefit your business. Social media is a powerful tool for reaching people, but it's good to weigh the pros and cons. On the plus side, it's a great way to connect with a broad audience, build your brand, and engage directly with customers. However, it can also be time-consuming, and if not done right, it may not yield the desired results. Planning is another key element. It's essential to know what your intentions are and have a detailed proposal that outlines your goals and how you plan to achieve them. This helps keep you focused and ensures that you're moving in the right direction. Organization is about bringing together the right people and ideas in a logical order. Surrounding yourself with influencers who can help push your tasks forward is a smart move. These are the people who can help you spread the word and reach more potential customers. When it comes to marketing your brand, think about how you want to reach your intended audience. Will you go for direct advertisement, like email marketing, or indirect methods, like influencer partnerships? Communication with your consumers is key—how you present your product or service can make all the difference. Influence plays a big role in building strategies to reach various communities. Having a solid framework for this helps you connect with people in meaningful ways. And of course, knowing your customers is crucial. You want to balance their needs and wants while figuring out what will make them interested in your product or services. Cash flow is the lifeblood of your business. It's important to ensure that your business is generating enough revenue to keep things running smoothly. Also, think about how you can create a win-win situation with your shareholders—how can they benefit from your success, and how can you benefit from their support? Having the right attitude is so important, especially when things don't go as planned. Maintaining a positive outlook, even when things seem out of reach, can help you push through challenges. Ultimately, taking responsibility for your organization and all its efforts is key. It's important to understand what makes your product or service stand out from the competition. What do you offer that others don't? Owning this uniqueness will help you carve out your space in the market. This advice comes from years of trial and error and experience in finding what works and what doesn't. These are great places to start when thinking about entrepreneurial goals and carving out your own success in business with excellence in mind at all times. Now let's dive into ministry. There is a stigma surrounding places of worship, and it's been written that we should not forsake the assembly of the House of God (church). It is on the rise that people are refusing to come together. We have gotten into this mode of doing our own thing because of corrupt leadership. Leaders in church are not providing any guidance or hope in the house of God because of self-serving motives and selfishness. This has to change. The house of God should be like a hospital, always open, always welcoming, filled with kindness, gentleness, and grace. We have to remember that usually when people come to church, they are hurting and looking for something they lack, needing an escape provided. We have gotten too comfortable "serving God" from our couches and computer screens.

And I believe strongly that God wants to bring healing to families, marriages, and people with mental torment, fear, and suicidal thoughts. People are searching for the love and guidance that church leadership is supposed to provide. There is so much skepticism surrounding who can be trusted in the church. There is a responsibility that people who hold leadership positions must take seriously. But ultimately, we have to put our faith and trust in God alone. God will always have your back. We have to do things the right way, the godly way, and He will always fight for us. I believe a lot of times we get disappointed in church settings because we are focusing too much on people and what people say or do. When you go to church, it is to give God glory. This thing is two-fold. Yes, leadership is important; we need leadership. The right kind of leadership, of course, but what your life depends on is your personal relationship with God. If you search for a leader and don't find the qualities I've listed in this chapter, take that as it is probably not the fit for you. We become so easily annoyed and hypercritical that we lose sight of what is really important. You are never going to find a perfect church filled with perfect people; it doesn't exist. These things I have observed in the African American church; I realize that other cultures worship differently, and their belief systems are set up a different way, but there is a structured protocol that we all must follow regardless of how each one of us worships. We are fundamentally obligated to worship God Almighty. He said in the word that every knee shall bow and every tongue shall confess that He is the ONLY living God. We are collectively as a people continuing to not see the breakthrough we need in our lives because we are focused on the wrong things and not what truly matters. To close out this chapter, I want to highlight some key things to keep in our hearts and minds regarding our relationship with God. And remember this: no matter what your culture or background is, or if you were born a leader or if you have worked hard and long to become one, we all have the same script to follow. A relationship with God is deeply personal and starts with intimacy, which is about how close you feel to God and what He means to you. It's worth asking yourself if you really know God on a personal level. A balanced prayer life is key, where discipline and consistency in your prayer habits help you stay connected. Studying the Word of God is another critical aspect—it's important to assess your level of understanding and how often you engage with the scriptures. Your love language with the Father reflects how you relate to God, and it's vital to understand your own existence concerning Him. Trust is foundational in this relationship, so it's critical to identify how much you truly trust God. Lastly, faith plays a significant role—faith is about taking chances, believing in what you cannot see, and recognizing that it is the substance that sustains you. Together, these elements form a meaningful and fulfilling relationship with God.

Chapter Eight

Unstoppable

After reflecting on the hardships I've suffered in my life, I realized that my testimony couldn't simply be a recounting of events but rather a guiding light for other women to lean on. This is why I chose to write and will continue to share my story–to serve as a beacon of hope. I've learned to be diligent, steadfast, and unstoppable to persevere both mentally and physically. While I've always possessed the mindset to keep pushing forward, there have been moments of doubt or exhaustion when giving up seemed tempting. Yet, the idea of being unstoppable equates to being unhindered; it reminds us that we can't stay stuck, and we can't afford to have missteps. Instead, we must embrace the unlimited possibilities before us, winning from within, and finding a more defined direction in our lives. When you take on the attitude of being unstoppable, something remarkable happens; the obstacles that once seemed insurmountable become just another phase of growth. I'm sure others can identify with some of the things in this chapter that have tried to stifle you, but this is where the power of pausing to develop personal affirmations for us and taking bold stands becomes necessary. We cannot allow ourselves to be confined by the expectations or judgments of others. Only moving forward from here, we transform our challenges into fuel, driving us to greater heights. That's why I titled my book "I'm That Girl"–it boldly declares that I refuse to let life's obstacles hold me back, and I encourage other women to do the same. Long ago, I had to make a choice; I simply will not purely exist. I am determined to thrive. I am being reminded in writing this chapter, about all the things in my life that I have had to endure that would attempt to stop my momentum but failed. We must always maintain our momentum of striving. More than anything else, it is the fact that I am so widely misunderstood. By my family, peers, and even my children. I have always just been different. People so often decide to judge and treat badly anything or anyone different than them. Rather than trying to understand what they didn't know or like about me, that is what happened. I have had to plunge myself through so much heartbreak simply because I am different. Starting very early on at home with my siblings. They treated me badly, left me out of things, bullied me, mislabeled and misjudged me, and constantly rejected me because I was different than them. I was always the oddball out; sometimes even my parents resented me because I was not like the others. I had goals and ambitions that were ignored, even laughed at. I often felt all alone, and rejection became a force that felt evil to me; it began to take root in me, and I started to act out to get the attention I was starving for within my family. These people who were supposed to love and accept me before anyone else made me feel unwanted and unimportant. It was as if I didn't even matter, nor did my feelings. Being so misunderstood and misjudged began to make me behave in ways I am not proud of. When we let others and the way they treat us dictate how we act and live, an identity crisis is around the corner. I went through a crisis of identity in my younger years because I had nobody to shake me and tell me my value was not dependent on how others viewed me or how they treated me. I had to find that out on my own. After all the rejection and mistreatment I went through with my siblings, I chose to be someone else for a time, yearning for acceptance and approval. When I started to act out and hang with the wrong crowd, I got sucked into a way of life that, deep down, I knew was not for me. I lost myself for a little while, yes. But I started to get more and more uncomfortable and uneasy around sin and things of a sinful nature. It started to be overwhelming–that feeling of conviction and shame. I knew I had forsaken who I truly was and wanted to be. I didn't belong with the bad crowd; I knew it. Somewhere along the way, I made a choice. To be me unapologetically. At some point, I recognized that the way my siblings and family were treating me reflected their hearts and the ugliness was inside of them, not inside of me. So, I refused to become what they wanted me to become. After nearly having my identity stolen away from me, I decided to be true to myself no matter what anyone thinks. I came back to my goals and was persistent in my pursuit of them. I made my mom pay attention, and after many forced conversations with her about what I desired to do and achieve, she began to see me and help me with the things I needed to do to feel better about myself and who I wanted to become. I became relentless in the pursuit of my goals. I made myself visible again, my true self. You see, it is okay to have moments or times in your life that you feel like you cannot continue, or you may lose yourself for a second. What is not okay or acceptable is giving up. You must not stay there. All that heartbreak and loneliness taught me to never change who you are or how you behave to please others. I have tried it; I have lost myself in the opinion and rejection of others, and it got me nowhere but more heartache. People will never be satisfied; they will always seek to tear down what they don't understand. I will never be a people pleaser. I could have stayed lost in my own family and just crumbled and withered away, but instead I learned from the hurt and the pain. I used it to make me strong. I didn't let it break me entirely; I used it to build up my character, and it made me treat people better. Don't ever stop, no matter who approves or doesn't. I had to choose to separate myself from anyone who refused to celebrate me, family included. I still to this day remain separated from my family by choice. I have come to understand that they just do not get my differences. I refused to be hindered by my family's opinion of me, let alone anyone else's. Even when my heart has been disappointed so many times because people refuse to let their mindset shift when talking or dealing with me. I can see it in the middle of a conversation; they have already made up their mind to judge and reject. Most people make their minds up about you before even knowing or understanding your intentions; it is so sad. My family was only the beginning; I have been misjudged, lied about, slandered, and gossiped about so much. And of course, it is heart-wrenching because I know my heart is pure towards people. I know that I don't wish anyone any harm. I know my character and how I treat people. What is even worse is that when people know and realize you are unbreakable and unstoppable, they still will try repeatedly to break you. I refuse. I cannot and will not be stopped by anyone. I have realized many people tend to misinterpret my language, and the things I speak are so deep sometimes that it is hard to find anyone to echo me or connect with me on that level, which can make me feel alone at times. I have even thought to myself, "Who is speaking for you?" The answer has always been God. I rely on him, and I keep moving. Even in my motherhood, my children mislabeled me as "mean" because I was strict with them. That hurt me, but it didn't stop me from being the kind of mother that was required of me. It didn't stop me from loving them fully and unconditionally. That label sure didn't stop me from trying to help them achieve excellence in their lives. It took many different conversations with my kids to break down that label and barrier; little by little, we broke through that misunderstanding. When my marriage didn't work out the way I envisioned it, I did not let that stop me from opening my heart to love and marriage again. Of course, I had a period of healing and feeling all the emotions that can sprout from a failed union, but I did not let myself stay there. To be completely honest with you, sometimes I feel forsaken in my personal life. I have yet to find a man of God that can lead and match my drive, energy, and ambition. In my past regarding dating, I have been mistreated because of the depth of insecurities that a lot of men operate from, which would cause me to have to defend myself. I have not come across a male figure in my life who has been able to compliment my leadership qualities and abilities. I know by speaking to women on a constant basis that many, married or single, are struggling with the same issue. Men not living up to what is required to actually lead. There is much ego and pride in a lot of men, and they are simply not up to the challenge and do not have what it takes to counterbalance a woman with such strength who is sure of herself. This part of my life has become lonely at times, but I keep on moving. I have come to rely on God for everything. I turn to him for companionship even when I may feel forsaken in those moments. That is what we have to understand fully. Despite how any of the things we go through in life make us feel, it's only for a moment. Life is composed of many moments, good or bad. But moments pass, and another challenge or struggle may be on the horizon, but understand that it is only a moment, and it will pass. Keep moving forward. We must understand as women the depth of the word unstoppable. What it truly means to be that force that cannot be stopped. It takes faith, courage, bravery, and strength. It takes knowing your ability to fight vigorously against disarray. Women, being unstoppable, we must show up for ourselves. Presence, SPEAKS. I have spoken with so many women from different walks of life that I have had to encourage them to keep going regardless of what they are going through looks like. We must keep moving and never give up. We must weather the storm, any storm, with grace. And if you mess up and make a mistake, pick yourself up off the ground, dust off your shoulders, and begin again. Become a finisher; no matter how many times you have to begin again, finish and finish well. Push yourself, even when you do not feel like it. Finish what you start! Elevate your mindset to believing fully that you can do it, whatever it is. Because I promise you, you can. Put in place your own personal plan of action and see it through. Even if you have to do it alone. When you create a habit of seeing things through and continuing to go on, no matter what the situation may look like, it builds a supernatural strength, courage, and confidence in yourself that will push and guide you through everything in your life. All of the things that tried to prohibit me from being who I was meant to be or accomplishing what I set out to do only refined me and made me better in the end. I am proud of myself today; I am happy with my accomplishments. I am overjoyed with the relationships I have fostered, and I have people that love and accept me for who I am and nothing else. We must continue to empower each other to become mentally resilient, never settle for less, and pursue our happiness while standing up for ourselves. Being unstoppable means embodying a level of resilience that allows us to remain steadfast in the face of challenges. I've had to make significant changes in my life to maintain mental stability and stay true to myself. I've learned that our approach to life shapes our destiny, and despite the obstacles others may try to place in our path, we must never allow ourselves to be limited. Our upbringing plays a significant role in shaping who we become, but even if we weren't given the tools or support we needed, we could still rise to become our own champions. Let's embrace our journey, overcome adversity, and empower each other to reach our fullest potential. We can become more of conquerors when we remain unmovable. I simply don't know the word 'stop'. I have always been that girl who kept moving, being a finisher in things and personal goals I set for myself. Winning is contagious. Surround yourself with winners, and you will become one as well. When I reflect on my life, I think about many occurrences where I had to keep fighting. One of them was that even though I was overlooked or resisted by others because of my ability to tell them the truth or get them to see themselves, it only fueled my desire to keep going and being me. I have been given something special to keep making things happen, no matter what obstacles or delays may come, from those who don't want to see you thrive—and that can be anyone. I am constantly taking notes and applying new things to my life to stay refreshed, renewed, and focused on being that woman who doesn't let life setbacks or drama from others slow me down. One thing that is certain is that I am a risk-taker. Taking risks and taking chances, utilizing my faith, so that it can take me the distance. If you want to be unstoppable, you will have to start taking risks and being completely sure that no matter the outcome, you will be okay. The willingness to try and learn by any means necessary is an important quality when you want to persevere and succeed in your life. That bravery will be rewarded; you have to believe that with all your heart. One way or another, things have a way of working out in your favor when your heart is in the right state and position. As a woman, keep in mind that finding purpose and your own willingness is something you can always depend on to make it in life. Unstoppable is a mindset; women unmasking it together can be powerful if we become one voice. We must learn to rely on each other for shared strength. We are so much stronger when we are unified. When women band together to accomplish things, they become unstoppable. We have to continue to forge solid relationships and build community with each other. Just think, if we were to unify and depend on one another for strength and courage found through our own suffering, the forces of darkness that try to silence us would be defeated. 'Unstoppable', the word itself standing alone, can give us superpowers—not imaginary, but real in the sense of our ability to accomplish anything in life. Affirmations are powerful tools that can shape our mindset and drive us toward our goals. Each of these affirmations embodies a spirit of resilience, determination, and self-belief, which are essential for becoming truly unstoppable. "I will overcome" speaks to the strength to face and conquer challenges, while "I believe" reinforces the importance of self-confidence and faith in one's abilities. "I will start my business" is a declaration of initiative and entrepreneurial spirit, and "I will not be held back" emphasizes the resolve to break free from limitations. "I will free my heart" highlights the importance of emotional liberation and authenticity. "I will never give up" is a testament to perseverance, and "I will have vision" underscores the necessity of foresight and planning. "I will persevere" reiterates the commitment to enduring through difficulties, and "I will always give myself a standing ovation" encourages self-recognition and celebration of one's achievements. Finally, "I will win" encapsulates the ultimate goal of success and triumph. Together, these affirmations create a powerful narrative of empowerment and unstoppable momentum.

I WILL OVERCOME.

I BELIEVE.

I WILL START MY BUSINESS.

I WILL NOT BE HELD BACK.

I WILL FREE MY HEART.

I WILL NEVER GIVE UP.

I WILL HAVE VISION.

I WILL PERSEVERE.

I WILL ALWAYS GIVE MYSELF A STANDING OVATION.

I WILL WIN.

UNAPOLOGETIC | UNSTOPPABLE

Chapter Nine

Offense

Offense is on the rise in our society in many sectors because we simply have our emotions working overtime. The lens through which I view this thing called "offense" is BROAD. It operates in our lives in many ways. Sometimes it needs to be addressed and viewed with both close examination and distant reflection. In other words, you may have times when you have to look at it closely, and other times it needs to be looked at from a distance. Let's talk about offense in-depth to gain a clear understanding of what we are dealing with, as it is one of those things that can either make or break a person. Being THAT girl will require you to deal with offense in a different capacity than most, so it is very important to take a closer look at the many ways that offense can show itself. Offense is often rooted in misguided emotions. Offense can be a disease that eats at the core of our soul if we allow it to. Offense can hide itself all throughout and within our physicality—in our elbows, in our feet, in our toes. It can hide in our ears, in our mouths, in our wombs, as women. Most commonly, offense will hide away in our eyes and will blind you spiritually and naturally so that nothing is going in and nothing is coming out; you're just perpetually offended. Offended, blinded, and any possibility of growth; stunted. When offense hides in our bodies, it's waiting for a moment to manifest. Waiting for an opportunity to make us ill. I feel this is why many women experience so much disease and illness in their bodies because an offense has taken hold and festered into something ugly. Offense can breed a certain type of misery that can make you feel like there is no escape. Resentment can then set up an insult that can turn into bitterness and hatred. Make no mistake—the root of bitterness breeds offense. It goes literally both ways: offense unchecked causes bitterness to take root, and bitterness, when left unchecked, is the root of that offense; if not dealt with, will then cause offense to take root in you. Then before you know it, you live in a state of constantly being offended, resulting in a truly miserable existence because it will poison every aspect of your life to make you bitter and resentful toward everything. We can get to a point where we become so easily offended that we fail to understand anything. Offense will have you operating from a place of victim mentality and self-righteous behavior. And that self-righteous attitude will make you feel like you are always right about everything. You will remain unteachable. You will always be looking for fault in everyone else; you will never see anyone else as right. Your viewpoint will stay distorted so that you are unable to see things clearly. You will repeatedly respond from a place where you feel you always have to stick up for yourself. Constant fight mode, no rest, no peace, fatigue will set in. You'll end up being isolated and feeling abandoned because it is so hard to love a person who is constantly offended. Like most things, there are different levels or degrees of offense, and it can manifest on various levels, each impacting your life and happiness differently. Let's talk about those levels. Minor offenses are everyday annoyances or misunderstandings, like rude comments or a slight inconvenience. While they might sting momentarily, they usually don't have a lasting impact unless you dwell on them. Moderate offenses involve more significant issues, like a friend betraying your trust or a colleague taking credit for your work. These offenses can hurt more deeply and may require time and effort to resolve. Major offenses are serious grievances, like a betrayal by a loved one, discrimination, assassination of your character, people lying about you, and abuse. Major offenses can profoundly affect your emotional and mental well-being and sometimes even require professional help and deliverance to heal. Those major offenses are the dangerous ones; these are the things that will cut so deeply that it may take longer to heal from, and often we get stuck because of those major offenses. I want to talk about a deeply personal situation I experienced with my family. I can close my eyes and recall it like it was only yesterday; it was so deeply painful that it definitely would fall under that major offense category. The behavior my family showcased after the tragic loss of my brother Jaques last year offended me completely. The day he passed as a result of a car accident, I was running errands on the way to work, and I had to run in to a tire shop and was sort of rushing because I had to get to my job. I received the devastating news in the middle of the chaos of my daily routine. That part is important to understand because when the call came through, I had a very limited reaction with no emotion. Remember, I was rushing around trying to finish up my errands and get to work as I was running late. I think that combined with the initial shock caused me to react slowly. Then, like an instant flash across my mind, I quickly remembered the dream I had had the night before. I then realized God had prepared me for that very moment. When I woke up that morning, I had no idea what the dream meant, as many dreams are confusing at first. But as it all unfolded, in that very specific moment, it all came together and made sense. Like a divine math equation solving itself in front of me. Because all of it was registering in my mind, my reaction on the phone with a family member was filled with empty silence. She began to pray to herself. I called out her name and said, "He's gone." She quickly had a fiery rebuttal, but what she didn't realize was that I was actually responding from my perspective within the dream that I had. Of course, I had no intention of sounding cold or emotionless. But here's the thing—like we discussed earlier—a lot of people operate from that place of constant offense. They anticipate being offended by everyone and everything, so instead of responding from a place of grace or understanding, this person already had it in them to judge me and be offended by my response. The fact that I was silent for a moment was just enough to give this person the ammunition to find fault with me and be offended by my lack of an emotional response. Beware of people who look for a problem with everything. From that point forward, I was judged and labeled as cold and emotionless concerning the passing of my brother, which could not be further from the truth. In fact, I called my pastor screaming and crying that my brother was gone and that he was dead. The silence on the other end of that phone call was a stillness. The phone call with that family member in the silence was apprehension; it was judgment; it was tension. It was as if no matter what my reaction was on the phone with her, it would have been problematic. Now, I have never been one to be offended by much, except if it has to do with my children. There have been some occasions when I've pondered whether I truly felt offended by patterns of misguided heresy or not. But this situation turned into a storm of me being consistently misunderstood, mislabeled, and judged by my family, which hurt me to no end, especially during such a hard and sad time with losing my brother; of course, losing him affected me. Of course, it made me sad. Because I didn't react in the way they wanted me to in that moment, I was completely misunderstood, judged, and treated unfairly. This situation had me feeling offended because of the lies and the attack on my character, hearing something completely different than what I was saying, and judging me for mere moments of no tears, no loud shout, nor cry. This particular family member has always acted as if she was the glove, holding the family together. In reality, she is the problem and refuses to see it. My brother even said to me once about this relative, "They know no loyalty to anyone." I sat back during this experience and watched the lies, this scary level of deception, them being so deeply accusatory, and I was simply offended. This offense had me weeping for days, all the while grieving for my brother. I became so disappointed with the many lies told to each other about me and the manipulation, twisting the truth to fit their narrative. I literally had to cut off all communication with my family. I realized I always have seen them have no remorse, be full of hate and evil with a self-righteous attitude. I must tell my truth in this book because there is a level of freedom here, in these pages. Everyone has family demons; don't act like you don't. Stop being in denial. I'm

That Girl, and I will tell you the truth! I still have not talked to them, but once since then. I have had to completely separate myself from any toxic behavior. I decided I would much rather be a woman who stays free from toxicity, family or not. If they do not add value to your life and refuse to celebrate you and continue to hurt you, they need to go. Simple as that. Point and case. You are not required to be in anyone's life, whether they're friends, family, or colleagues; it is not a requirement to have them in your space; it simply is your choice. If it drains you, simply remove it. I was offended, and the hurt from the dagger penetrated through to my heart. I was so hurt by my family. I felt an emotion I had never felt before—something new. I have been through much, but this specific hurt was a new hurt. Falsely accusing me of something I did not do made me feel a way that was foreign. Deeply offended. This offense was trying to decapitate the lifeline that God had prepared for me to survive in this moment. Attack after attack kept coming, so when they didn't see me crumble like they have truly always wanted me to, I got a text from a member of the family saying, "You need to be ashamed of yourself for taking sides with Jacques Wife. I see you on Facebook, and I have discernment" Right at that very moment, it was one of the cruelest things she could have said to me. We had a few discussions before we left from pulling the plug on my brother, resulting in the fact that no one wanted to deal with his wife. So, I said I would. To me, it was not about us but about giving my brother the best home-going, which is what he deserved. After having been a professional sufferer and then getting caught up in unfruitful relationships in his life, my brother lived in a state of despair that put him before his premature death. This particular family member was not even present but is known for being a busybody in others' affairs. Now, I choose to do things God's way. I had to acknowledge the wife and do what she wanted to see happen at the funeral. Preacher selection, colors, etc. Everything that transpired was to be solidified with her signature. In this conversation, I attempted to give my family member a scenario about a matter close to her heart, trying to get her to see that she was thinking incorrectly. Only to find myself in a fight that I knew I would win. How can I say that? Because when you fight in righteousness, you fight right; winning is always the outcome. Never to be defeated. God will always be on your side. When we approach things in life with the right motives and intentions, offense will have you paralyzed in your thoughts. You can then become premeditated in doing wrong and find yourself in regrettable circumstances. This fight continued, and she told others I threw her situation in her face, which was an outright lie. When you are dealing with people who only hear with ears full of pride, sometimes you have to speak in parables. Jesus did it. I saw he was successful in showing folks their ways. I have many encounters with people who operate out of offense to discover that pride is at work in them; they don't know how to make better choices for themselves, so they sit stuck in offensive behavior. When you become THAT girl, you do not let others' dysfunction dictate how you respond to life and its challenges. Be the one that chooses the right way. As this story was unfolding, I began thinking, "Let me try and get some resolve in the situation by having one family member speak to the other one, in hopes of talking some sense into them possibly." She said to me, "I told her not to tell you about her business. She will use it against you." I was frozen and confused. She had never had that experience with me. Where does this stuff even come from? Well, the root of this problem with this person has always been envy. Envious of another person's strength. Sorry, I refuse to take part and will die free from the bondages of hell. I sat there listening to her speak untruths about so many things. I asked her if she was done after a moment of silence, and she said she was. My question to her was, "What is your problem with me? What is wrong? "Her actual reply was "nothing." She really actually said the word nothing. After all that, venom spewed from her mouth. Let me help you out. An attack is real when you are targeted to be something that you aren't; your adversary will try and make your family speak against you. How can my family say in one moment, "You're the strongest; you're the rock of the family." (Blank Stare) How can I be if you are blinded by your own opinion of me? How does that work? To draw from a well in me, and you say the water is dry. It makes zero sense to me. If someone is determined to be offended by you or dead set on doing things to offend you, there is nothing you can say or do to fix that; that is an issue with them, a personal problem, and you are only responsible for your side of the street being clean. The process to get through all of this was long, but I knew the fruit of their doings. I began to share my story with people I have in my life in hopes that they could relate, but they acted as if they could not understand where I was coming from. It was this whole act of dismay or clutching their pearls in judgment, which is also offensive. See, we can be offended for good reason. I felt justified in my offense in this situation; I did hurt for a while, but I refused to stay there and let it make me bitter. I will remain unstoppable. Even in offense, you should try that. Because this thing can go both ways. Yeah, Ottoweiss is a fighter, but always remains godly in those fighting moments. Understand that offense was designed to try and keep you from embracing new things in your future. Offense will sometimes attach to us like magnets. It will sometimes be a pain that feels like a knife in your heart that will be hard to pull out. We can find ourselves holding onto grudges and past hurts, allowing them to fester and grow within us. These feelings can cloud our judgment, influence our decisions, and hinder our progress. It's important to recognize when offense is taking root in our hearts and take proactive steps to address it. For me, the offense from my family's behavior during such a vulnerable time became a heavy burden. It affected my relationships, my peace of mind, and my ability to move forward. I had to learn to let go, to forgive, and to place my trust in God's plan for me. It was not easy, and it required deep introspection and a willingness to confront many uncomfortable truths. In moments of offense, we have to remember that only our reactions are within our control. We can choose to respond with grace and understanding, even when faced with hurtful words and actions. This doesn't mean we condone or accept mistreatment, but rather that we refuse to let it define us or dictate our future. As I continued to navigate my grief and the familial discord that followed, I leaned heavily on my faith. I found solace in prayer and scripture, drawing strength from the promises of God. Offense, while painful, can also be a catalyst for growth and transformation. It can lead us to greater self-awareness and a deeper reliance on divine guidance. Ultimately, offense is a tool of the enemy designed to disrupt our lives and our relationships. Offense, to me, is a weakness, a sign of a blackened heart that is fixed on seeing the negative. By recognizing its presence and choosing to respond with love and forgiveness, we can overcome its destructive influence. We must remain vigilant, guarding our hearts and minds against the corrosive effects of offense. Only then can we fully embrace the new things that God has in store for us, free from the chains of past hurts and misunderstandings. Holding onto offense can really take a toll on your mental health, often leading to anxiety, depression, and other related issues. It can drain your emotional energy, leaving you feeling exhausted and overwhelmed, which can impact your overall happiness and quality of life. In relationships, staying offended can create strain, leading to resentment and a lack of trust. This strain can also affect your physical health, with chronic stress from holding onto offense potentially causing high blood pressure and weakened immunity. If not addressed, offense can pave the way to bitterness, a state of chronic resentment and anger. Bitterness can cloud your judgment, making you see the world through a negative lens and affecting your decisions and interactions. It can also isolate you, pushing people away and leaving you feeling lonely. Furthermore, bitterness can hinder your personal growth, trapping you in a cycle of negativity and preventing you from moving forward and achieving your goals. I have chosen to embrace joy throughout my journey in life. I have made a conscious decision that offense will remain merely a byword in my vocabulary. At this stage in my life, I feel I have truly apprehended this concept. No longer will I allow others to distort my path or lead me toward self-destruction by refusing to acknowledge their own errors. I live in truth, not denial, and I recognize that offense is a constant state of denial that many people are enslaved to.

Chapter Ten

Be **Bold** About It!

Okay ladies, it's time to bring this thing home. The whole concept behind the inspiration for this project was and has always been to encourage you to become and live your very best life as "THAT girl." It was written carefully and specifically with you in mind, to inspire you to come to know yourself fully and embrace yourself completely. To fall in love with who you are, flaws and all. To use those flaws to challenge yourself in carrying out your destiny and living your truth, without apologies. This book was written to walk with you through a journey of self-discovery, self-realization, and ultimately self-love and acceptance. If you read with an open mind and heart, each chapter should have brought you closer to living a life full of purpose and passion. With each page, another layer of revelation knowledge uncovered all you need to guide you toward a life full of love, joy, happiness, peace, and power. Each chapter should have been a light that gets brighter with each word, illuminating the path leading us toward becoming "THAT girl." As we reach the final chapter of this journey, it's time to bring together all the lessons and insights we've explored. I realize I may have thrown a lot of information at you, and all of it together may seem overwhelming and like a lot of work, or maybe even difficult to process. I hate to break it to you, but being THAT girl and living your very best life is not an easy thing. It isn't simple; it isn't for the lazy or simple-minded kind of person. It is a lifestyle made up of many simple truths, but it is full of hard work and constant evolution and change. Don't get me wrong, a lot of the components and characteristics may come naturally to some, but if you are looking for an easy way to live out the rest of your existence without challenging yourself on a constant basis and challenging the way others view and treat you, I appreciate you getting this book and even more than that, finishing it. But this life may not be for you! I believe every woman has the capability of being THAT girl, unapologetic and unstoppable, living a full life of success and perseverance. But you gotta want it more than anything. You gotta know that you know that you know that you KNOW. You gotta be SURE of who you are and what you are capable of. You gotta be unwavering in your commitment to the betterment of yourself and those around you. You gotta be able to keep the momentum of excellence going throughout the duration of your life. This is not like a singular experience or so-called 'awakening' where you 'see the light' and you are changed and never have to do anything else again to maintain your sense of self. This lifestyle and manner of existence is to take the hard road almost always. The road that takes the most courage, the most bravery, and determination. The road that usually comes with the most challenging trials and the one where you face situations that would take the average person out. This is not for the faint of heart. This is about living relentlessly in your truth and doing it boldly. Let's talk about that—boldness. The actual definition of boldness is the willingness to act originally and to be innovative, to have confidence or courage. I am sure I have mentioned all three of those ideals all throughout this book because they are all vital to being THAT girl. I have always been a woman who walks in boldness in every aspect of my life, and that boldness has often been misconstrued and confused as arrogance or some kind of superiority complex. There has always been something in the depths of my being that calls me to be a woman who remains relentless in her stance about most things that I've had to encounter. Boldness exudes from my person all the time. I am not afraid to say what others won't. I have never been afraid to express myself. Sometimes my boldness was living out the quiet part of boldness—out loud. Now, don't let that go over your head. Don't complicate it. It takes a level of boldness to remain quiet at times when others feel the need to be the loudest one in the room; silence often speaks volumes. Just like it takes courage to speak up, it also takes courage to remain calm and quiet in certain situations. We cannot remain silent about all things though; women often hide themselves in a layer of silence when they have been abused or raped. We cannot hide ourselves from those unfortunate things that may have happened to us. We must boldly confront them by speaking those things out loud. Women often confuse silence about those horrible things as strength, which is why I constantly encourage women to express themselves. I challenge my mentees and the women that I counsel to speak out about those traumatic events because not only does it liberate you from those things that will try and put a hold on you, but it also will inspire and incite hope in other women that may be going through those things in secret to get help, which will transform their lives, and your story may be the catalyst for someone's life to be saved and changed for the better. Our stories and testimonies are meant for a greater purpose than just filling up space in a conversation. When we boldly share our struggles and those moments of brokenness and pain, we relate to other women and break down walls of shame and guilt that prevent us from living our best lives and being our best selves. Outward expression brings about redemption. Women tend to get comfortable with living in that shame and silence for fear of being judged or looked down upon. Sometimes women are hiding from themselves. Our secrets will make and keep us sick. Secrets will literally bring about infirmities in our bodies and severe mental anguish. Women who are abused and taken advantage of tend to internalize everything and make what they are going through somehow their own fault. We keep giving power to those things that have hurt us when we keep all of it on the inside. Come out of hiding and out of the shadows. We remain at a crossroads when we refuse to bring those things out of the darkness. Come out of the crossroads and darkness and step into the light! You can experience freedom when you liberate yourself from everything you keep bottled up inside. We have to boldly remove ourselves from that victim mentality. Rehearsing victim mentality makes us enemies to ourselves. I have witnessed first-hand women unburdening themselves from the things they refuse to talk about that keep them bound. That moment when the light returns to their eyes and the darkness starts to dissipate is glorious and brings me personally so much joy. It is the moment when they realize healing is indeed possible and that they don't have to live in fear or shame anymore. That is when it all starts, when we can be honest with ourselves and open about what has hurt us and begin the process of overcoming. This takes an immense amount of boldness and courage. Our testimony is so powerful. Sometimes all it takes is a listening ear and a willingness to be bold, if only for a moment at first. The ability to be honest and open about traumatic experiences doesn't always happen all at once, but when you give yourself a chance, the floodgates will open, and you will see that complete freedom from those things is possible. One thing is for certain: making bold moves changes the trajectory of your life, providing a whole new meaning to who you have allowed yourself to be. Boldness IS courage. Being bold is an ongoing conversation that is never-ending because there is always something to talk about when it comes to outward expressions of yourself. This thing is not imaginary; it is reality. Ladies, we have to face US because we are our own worst enemy. We are the ones preventing ourselves from being THAT girl and living our best possible lives. We have to tell our story; that's why it's so important to express yourself. You don't want to have holes in your story, and the holes stem from self-intimidation. Quit hiding from the very thing you need to release. It takes boldness to admit you have made wrong decisions and courage to try and rectify those mistakes. Let me also say this: living for extended periods of time with sadness and grief will allow your flesh to override what you already know to be not right. Meaning that when you experience loss of some kind, your mind will make excuses and tell you lies about fault, and guilt will fortify itself in your heart. So, you end up living with this heavy weight on yourself that will keep you stuck and in a place of constant regret and cause self-loathing and sometimes self-harm. A lot of women admire my boldness because I will say what they won't say or are afraid to say. I have gotten many women to face themselves and realize that making the wrong choices for their lives, that they are settling for less and ignoring their inner voice speaking to them and for them. It takes boldness to not settle. Some women end up marrying the wrong man and having children with the wrong man because they ignored all of the warning signs—the red flags that were right there—telling them to go left, and they deliberately go right. We do that because we have allowed our inadequacies to do our thinking for us instead of daring to boldly think differently and move differently. Taking risks requires boldness, always. I have always had a reason to be able to express myself in almost every setting. And the push has always been the knowledge that's within that keeps me expressing myself with boldness. I have never felt like I didn't have a voice to be heard. I'm also not ever afraid to say no! I have had to walk away from dysfunction. I love myself enough to walk away from things that would wreak havoc in my life. And I have never lost a battle, because my heart is not wicked. The matters of the heart dictate how we carry ourselves and how we operate. We must boldly confront what we carry in our hearts. Boldness might be the most important aspect of living your life as THAT girl, which is why every chapter in this book, every topic, and every theme encapsulates some form of boldness. To be bold is to embrace your true identity. In "True Identity," we delved into the importance of self-discovery and being true to yourself despite the obstacles and trauma we face.

Boldness means standing firm in who you are, regardless of any outside expectations or pressures. In "Fearlessly Breaking Barriers," we discussed the power of confidently shattering glass ceilings and facing challenges with strength and courage. Boldness is about taking risks, pushing boundaries, and not being afraid to fail. It's about being a force that cannot be stopped. "Suicide" was a deeply personal chapter that highlighted the courage it takes to live despite wanting to die. Boldness is finding the strength to continue, to seek help, and to embrace life even in the darkest moments. It's about being vulnerable and honest about our struggles. In "Intimidation/ Manipulation," we explored how people can use these tactics to tear others down. Boldness is about resisting these negative behaviors and choosing to uplift and support one another instead. It's about being a woman of integrity and strength. "Competitive Jealousy" taught us the importance of celebrating others rather than comparing ourselves to them. Boldness is recognizing that another woman's success does not diminish our own. It's about building and maintaining your own community of support and encouragement. "Women In Leadership" highlighted the challenges and responsibilities of women in positions of power. Boldness is leading with confidence, compassion, and resilience. It's about being a role model and paving the way for future generations. In "Unstoppable," we learned about the perseverance and determination required to be "THAT girl." Boldness is never giving up, no matter how tough the journey gets. It's about pushing through obstacles and staying focused on our goals. "Offense" reminded us how easily we can become bitter and resentful. Boldness is about letting go of offense, choosing forgiveness, and living a life of peace and fulfillment. It's about not allowing negativity to hold us back. Boldness is the thread that ties all these chapters together. It takes courage to live authentically, to face challenges head-on, and to support and uplift others. Ultimately, I wrote this book to challenge your insecurities and areas of low self-esteem. Timidity should not be in our life's vocabulary; it simply breaks down our ability to soar, be proactive, and be outgoing in our personality. I believe we all have a level of boldness that we just haven't tapped into. That's why we need to familiarize ourselves with ourselves—get to know you. Girl, why have you put limits on YOURSELF? Pause and ask yourself that question, and then you answer it. We live in a world that often tells women to be quiet and reserved, but it's time to embrace boldness. Fear and insecurities can hold us back, but changing our mindset can unlock a life of tenacity, self-discovery, and unapologetic living. Fear is a powerful emotion that can make us timid and hesitant. It whispers doubts and magnifies insecurities, convincing us that we're not enough. This fear often stems from past experiences, expectations from society, and internalized beliefs. But to live boldly, we must confront and overcome these fears. Consider the story of Rosa Parks, who faced her fears head-on and ignited a movement by simply refusing to give up her seat. Her boldness teaches us that courage can spark significant change. Insecurities are deeply rooted in us, often fueled by comparisons and negative self-talk.

Changing our mindset is critical. We need to shift from a place of self-doubt to one of self-belief. Embrace the mantra: "Be bold about it." This means living our lives with courage, pursuing our dreams with determination, and not letting fear dictate our actions. Practical steps to embrace boldness include starting each day with positive affirmations to build self-confidence, visualizing your goals and the bold steps you need to take to achieve them, and surrounding yourself with people who encourage and uplift you. Being bold requires tenacity. It's about digging deep, getting to know ourselves, and befriending our inner selves. We must cultivate resilience, understanding that setbacks are part of the journey. Whether it's a failed marriage, a miscarriage, or the pain of making new friends after being hurt, we must not be afraid to start again. Change is inevitable, and fearing it only holds us back. We must embrace change as an opportunity for growth. Taking the limits off ourselves means breaking free from self-imposed restrictions. It's about being open to new experiences and challenges. Embrace new opportunities by saying yes to new experiences, even if they scare you, commit to lifelong learning and personal growth, and develop the ability to adapt to new situations with a positive mindset. Boldness is very much about expression. We should not be afraid to share our feelings and be who we are. Hurt often causes us to withdraw and become timid, fearing negative responses from the world. But our feelings are valid and expressing them is a form of strength. Living unapologetically means being true to ourselves and not conforming to others' expectations.

Exercises like journaling can help you better understand and express your feelings; practicing public speaking can build confidence; and engaging in creative activities like art, music, or writing can serve as a form of self-expression. Living boldly is a journey of self-discovery and empowerment. It's about facing our fears, changing our mindset, and embracing our true selves. By being bold, we can live a life full of purpose, joy, and fulfillment. Living boldly and loving loudly are intertwined journeys that begin with the most important relationship you'll ever have —the one with yourself. Women often face societal pressures and expectations that can cloud their sense of self-worth and identity. However, embracing your true self and loving yourself fiercely are the keys to unlocking a life of fulfillment and joy. Firstly, prioritize self-discovery. This means taking the time to understand who you are, what you want, and what you need. We have to try and engage in introspective activities such as journaling, meditation, or simply spending time alone in nature. These practices can help you tune into your inner voice, away from the noise and opinions of others. Remember, self-discovery is an ongoing process. Be patient with yourself as you peel back the layers and reveal your true essence. Next, cultivate self-love. This isn't just about pampering yourself, although that can be part of it. True self-love is about treating yourself with the same kindness, compassion, and respect that you offer to those you care about. It's about acknowledging your worth, setting healthy boundaries, and not settling for less than you deserve. Practice positive affirmations and challenge negative self-talk. Surround yourself with people who uplift and support you, and distance yourself from those who drain your energy or undermine your confidence. Working hard to find and learn about yourself is necessary. Pursue your passions and interests, even if they seem unconventional or daunting. Take risks and step out of your comfort zone. Every new experience and challenge you embrace contributes to your growth and self-understanding. Don't be afraid to make mistakes; they are valuable learning opportunities that bring you closer to your true self. Falling in love with yourself involves celebrating your uniqueness. Embrace your quirks, flaws, and imperfections—they are what make you who you are. Practice gratitude for your body, your mind, and your spirit. Appreciate the journey you've been on and the strength you've shown. When you love yourself deeply, you set a powerful example for others and attract love and respect in return. Living boldly means being unapologetically authentic. Speak your truth, even if your voice shakes. Stand up for what you believe in, and don't be afraid to take a stand, even when it's unpopular. Boldness is about being brave enough to show the world your true self without fear of judgment or rejection. Loving loudly is about expressing your love openly and fearlessly. This includes loving yourself, loving others, and loving life. Share your feelings and emotions freely. Tell the people in your life how much they mean to you. Engage in acts of kindness and generosity. Love loudly by spreading positivity and joy wherever you go. Ultimately, to live boldly and love loudly is about embracing life with open arms and an open heart. It's about being courageous, taking risks, and pursuing your dreams with passion and determination. It's about loving yourself so deeply that you an example of light and inspiration to others. So, embark on this journey with confidence and grace, knowing that you are worthy of all the love and happiness the world has to offer. By being bold, we can live a life full of purpose, joy, and fulfillment. So, let's take the leap and be bold about it. I encourage you to take one bold step today, whether it's speaking up in a meeting, starting a new project, or reaching out to someone you have been hesitant to contact. To be "THAT girl" is to embody boldness in every aspect of our lives. It's about being unapologetically ourselves, breaking barriers, overcoming struggles, resisting negativity, celebrating others, leading with confidence, persevering with determination, and letting go of offense. As we conclude this journey, remember that being bold is not just an action but a way of life. Embrace it, live it, and be unapologetically "THAT girl."

UNAPOLOGETIC | UNSTOPPABLE